BIRD
TRACKS

A Field Guide to British Species

T0386301

BIRD TRACKS

A Field Guide to British Species

JOHN RHYDER
AND DAVID WEGE

The
History
Press

*'A wonderful book that shares rare knowledge in a clear and focused way.
I love it.'*
– Tristan Gooley, author and natural navigator.

First published 2024

The History Press
97 St George's Place, Cheltenham,
Gloucestershire, GL50 3QB
www.thehistorypress.co.uk

Text © John Rhyder, 2024
Text and illustrations © David Wege, 2024

British Library Cataloguing in Publication Data.
A catalogue record for this book is available from the British Library.

ISBN 978 1 80399 170 2

Typesetting and origination by The History Press.
Printed and bound in Great Britain by TJ Books Limited, Padstow, Cornwall.

Trees for Lıfe

CONTENTS

FOREWORD BY NICK BAKER

Everything leaves a trace, from beetles to badgers. It's not just about footprints, either. It can be hair, feathers, eggshells, strands of silk, feeding signs, droppings or even scent.

Birds are no exception. In some ways, they make life 'easy' for the naturalist – they leave distinctive, quite specific and relatively large clues. Evidence of their lives can take the form of nests, feathers (for which there are several excellent field guides), pellets, droppings, feeding signs and eggshell fragments. This makes them much more user-friendly than mammals and invertebrates in many respects.

However, when it comes to their tracks and footprints, things start to get confusing. Other than their size, bird tracks can seem decidedly 'samey' to the untrained eye.

Compounding the difficulty in interpreting bird tracks are their wings! Due to the power of flight, bird tracks can turn up seemingly randomly. The bird can plop down and lift off again, leaving the tracker with a clue that is often disconnected from any other! Then, even if you get a good impression – a neatly registered track that shows precise detail – there is the problem of a distinct lack of reference books and field guides that are brave enough to tackle such things. Until now.

This book is an essential compendium for any serious naturalist – I love it. It represents an almost forensic analysis of the details of every British bird's footprints, some of which are the common and likely culprits of those starry indentations in a mud puddle or snow. Then there are those so unlikely to be encountered that you might question their inclusion in the book, such as the Great Bustard, Kingfisher, and even Gyrfalcon! That said, unlikely doesn't mean impossible, and somewhere in that sentence, along with the joyous minutia contained in these pages, lies the very magic of tracking, not to mention a sense of reassurance that comes with such a completest approach – this can only be achieved by those that know their stuff.

Foreword by Nick Baker

An almost pathological obsession with detail is exactly what you need to really get the most out of tracking. By assimilating physical clues you tell a part of a story, and in doing so, the tracker develops an even more intimate and satisfying relationship with the natural world around them.

What you have in your hand is a comprehensive bible of information you never really thought you needed, but you do, and you will use it. I guarantee you will find yourself scrutinizing the edges of puddles and river banks with a renewed interest – just looking for opportunities to put this book through its paces.

This is a deliciously unique book and a labour of love. It will sit on my shelf, an essential compendium of its kind and a testimony to the lengths the passionate will go to share their love of their subject.

– Nick Baker, 2024

PHOTO CREDITS

Our sincere thanks to everyone who helped us with track photos, all of which were used to draw the track illustrations and write our species descriptions, and some of which are included here in the book. Those that are used here are identified by the photographer's initials as follows:

Richard Andrews, RA
Robin Bowman, RB
Gavin Chambers, GC
Ian Dawson, ID
Judi Dunn, JD
Anja Eger, AE
Martin Gebhardt, MG
Stani Groeneweg, SG
Hein van Grouw, HVG
Howard Houlston, HH
Mimi Kessler, MK
Suzanne Kynaston, SK
Giny Kasemir, GK
Karen MacKelvie, KM
René Nauta, RN
Andrew Nightingale, AN
Paul Nightingale, PN
Antonio Pardo, AP
Aaldrik Pot, APt
Dan Puplett, DP
Mila Saunders, MSr
Miriam Schulz, MS
Liz Smith, LS
Paul Wernicke, PW

ACKNOWLEDGEMENTS

In addition to the photo contributors listed above, we would like to extend our thanks to all of the wonderful people who have helped us – often in diverse ways – with our research and pulling this book together. Thanks go to: Richard Andrews, Matt Binstead (British Wildlife Centre), Robin Bowman, Rob Brumfitt, Cambridge Animal Behaviour Lab, Gavin Chambers, Judi Dunn (Wildwood Trust), Anja Eger, Angel Javier España, Lea Eyre, Steve Fletcher, Martin Gebhardt, Stani Groeneweg, Hein van Grouw (The Natural History Museum), Hawk Conservancy Andover, Alex and Emma Hill (British Bird of Prey Centre), Howard Houlston, Mimi Kessler (Eurasian Bustard Alliance), Suzanne Kynaston (Wildwood Trust), Date Lutterop, Karen MacKelvie, Tony Martin, René Nauta, Paul Nightingale, Antonio Pardo, Aaldrik Pot, Dan Puplett, Isa Rössner, Mila Saunders, Miriam Schulz, Gabriel Sierra, Liz Smith, Kirsty Swinnerton (Kent Wildlife Trust), Hollie Weatherill (Wildwood Trust), Paul Wernicke.

ABOUT THE AUTHORS

John Rhyder is a tracker, naturalist, author and woodsman. He is certified as a Senior Tracker through CyberTracker conservation. He is also an evaluator for CyberTracker and both trains and assesses wildlife trackers in track and sign identification and trailing or following animals using their tracks. He is fascinated by the natural world and in traditional knowledge and, together with wildlife tracking, his work is centred around the skills that support interaction with and connection to nature. For more information about John's work and writing visit www.woodcraftschool.co.uk

David Wege developed a passion for birds, birdwatching and all things 'nature' in childhood – a passion that led to thirty-year career in international bird and biodiversity conservation with BirdLife International. More recently, and under the expert mentorship of his co-author, David has rediscovered tracking: learning to read and interpret the tracks and signs left by animals as they pass across the landscape. He has quickly reached Professional level in interpreting tracks and signs, and now teaches to share this engaging and connective art and science with as many people as possible. David is also a keen wildlife photographer and illustrator. For more information about his work, visit www.davidwegenature.uk

DEDICATION

For my part, I, John, would like to dedicate this book to my family, friends and fellow naturalists who, together with the natural world, make life so interesting. Also huge thanks to my co-author David for his patience and for forging ahead during the moments when I couldn't devote as much time to this project as I would have liked.

I, David, would like to thank the amazing sharing tracking community for exchanging ideas, discoveries and track photos, and helping us make this book rich with detail. For encouraging me to start illustrating tracks I would like to thank my Wildniswind (wildniswind.de) team, and especially Miriam Schulz for her encouragement throughout.

INTRODUCTION

BIRD TRACKS FOR TRACKERS AND BIRDWATCHERS

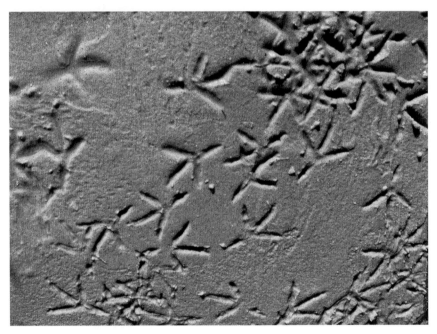

Collared Dove tracks.

As naturalists and trackers, we stare at a lot of mud and sand and dust, picking out the tracks to tell the stories of (most often) the mammals that passed by. This gives us an intimate understanding of their day-to-day lives even when the animal is long gone. Birds leave their tracks in these same places and – naturally – we want to be able to read their stories too. However, what we found with the bird tracks we were seeing was that we always came away with questions. Either we couldn't identify a track because the available books didn't help, or we were looking at a track we thought we knew – like Blackbird or Carrion Crow – and wondering what the difference was between this track and that of a Song Thrush or Rook, and again the books couldn't help.

So, this book came about principally to try and answer a question. What birds can be identified accurately to species level using only their tracks? Various publications in a number of countries have looked at bird tracks, and they have all helped to reveal the answers for some species, but none of them – in our view – have looked at the full range of birds of the British Isles and northern Europe in the kind of detail that we needed, and which we have attempted to present here.

Unlike our other mammalian friends, birds are easy to see and call or sing frequently, so the best way to discover which birds are in an area is by watching and listening, and that will always be the case. But, birds do leave tracks (and signs, such as feeding signs, feathers, nests and egg shells) that sometimes show us new things about the species (how it moves, what it's eating, where it's moulting and nesting), and occasionally give away their presence when we haven't seen or heard them. For example, the tracks of nocturnally active birds (such as Owls, Woodcock, Stone-curlew, etc.) can reveal their occurrence, feeding habits and ecology

Tawny Owl tracks.

Stone-curlew museum specimens.

during daylight when they are no longer active or even present. Waders in particular often use different sites to forage during the night, to roost at high tide or as traditional moulting areas (see Burton and Armitage, 2005, as an example), and tracking can help us discover those sites.

In addition to seeing and hearing birds, bird tracks are part of the evidence picture (along with other signs) and in this respect they enrich our understanding of what a species is doing, how it is living, and therefore also help strengthen our appreciation of that bird. It seems that within the birdwatching and ornithological community there is very little use of bird tracks and signs, and we feel that some might be missing out on an integral part of the story.

As trackers, we know that obvious features of the feet of certain birds allow us to make an accurate, species-level identification, but we wanted to see how far this concept could be taken. Would it be possible, for example, to tell Great Tit tracks from Nuthatch tracks, or House Sparrow from Chaffinch. With this question in mind, we also recognise that many species rarely spend much time on the ground, and still more are so small and light that they seldom leave tracks when they do venture down. Therefore we can ask the question: if a certain species only leaves infrequent, very hard-to-identify tracks, how useful is that knowledge in the real world? However, in exploring how far we can take bird track identification, we have looked for minute differences between tracks and studied their morphology in detail and feel we have shed some light on what is possible, what is not, and what may (or may not) have utility in the field. We are firm believers that tracking is about finding wildlife not just tracks, so utility is key!

COLLECTING TRACKS
AND GATHERING DATA

We started this bird track journey with lots of questions that the available literature could not answer for us. It was clear that we needed to gather first-hand data and find tracks for which we were 100 per cent positive of their identification. This meant taking a number of approaches.

Firstly, we did a lot of birdwatching! Watching birds along rivers, at puddles, on beaches and then searching for their tracks. Where there were birds but no tracking substrate, we set out track traps of sand (mostly of children's play sand, which is preferred because it is non-toxic), clay or anything really that would take the tracks of a bird. We placed track traps under bird feeders in gardens, out in the woods, by lakes – indeed, anywhere where we thought we had a chance of witnessing a bird landing. We then sat, watched and waited for birds to land, at which point we would rush out immediately before the tracks spoiled or got confused with another species.

We were lucky enough to gain access to some captive birds including Birds of Prey, Owls and Waterfowl. Waterfowl, in a private collection, were enticed across sand with the promise of food – the trick here being to try and do it one species at a time! In the case of the Birds of Prey and Owls, these were encouraged by their handlers to land on and move across track traps. The tracks were then photographed. We have also spent some time making plaster casts of the tracks, which gives yet another medium to study the accuracy of our findings.

We looked at and photographed the feet of birds in the hand (mist-netted under license for the purpose of ringing), and also the feet of museum specimens (at the British Natural History Museum in Tring). The museum specimens were useful in helping interpret what we were seeing in the tracks, determining the proportional length of toes, toe pad arrangements, length of nails, etc. They were also helpful for answering questions such as which species (Waders, Ducks, Gulls, etc.) have a Hallux and which do not? Is webbing present or not? Where does the webbing start and finish? That said, the dried-out feet of dead birds can't be used to anticipate what a track from the living bird would look like, so we have only used this information to interpret or confirm what we were seeing in the field.

Clockwise from top left: Little Tern museum specimens; A variety of track casts; Track traps; Comparing a track cast and its impression.

Clockwise from top left: Studying the feet of a captive White-tailed Eagle; Sand and clay around bird feeders to capture tracks; Track traps; Captive Birds of Prey helping us with track research.

We have referred to all the available published sources, a selection of which are shown below. Occasionally the photos published therein have

proven very helpful, and some of them are reproduced (with permission) here. Where we have struggled to find the tracks of certain species (primarily those that are more common in mainland Europe than here in Britain) we have requested track photos from other trackers, all of whom we would like to thank wholeheartedly for their generosity (and all of whom are listed in the Acknowledgements).

Right: Blue Tit in the hand.

Below: Bird tracks literature.

TRACK DRAWINGS

All the drawings in this book have been drawn electronically on a tablet using the free app Sketchbook. Essentially, they have been traced from track photos – following their features and shadows precisely. The app allows for multiple photos to be used (in separate layers), so each drawing is (most often) a composite of features from multiple track photos. One single track photo rarely shows all the features that we ideally want to illustrate, so merging features from multiple photos has hopefully created an accurate 'average' representation of a particular species' track. What becomes clear when tracing track photos is that even tracks from the same individual bird in the same substrate can present differently, with toe angles varying dramatically and features (such as nails, toe ends, Hallux, Metatarsal pad) showing and not showing. In spite of this, we have tried to show the most common presentation in the track drawings. It's worth keeping in mind, however, that the fewer photos we have had to work from, the greater the chance that the drawing might not be the perfect average we were striving for.

Perfect image of a Blackbird track.

A few brief words about track photos. If you ever decide to draw animal tracks from photos you will quickly find that the quality of the photo is paramount. A good track photo requires a good track – a track that is in substrate that holds the details and is not too deep. The photograph needs to be taken from directly above the track, ideally in neutral light (with not too much strong shadow). And a scale of some sort in the photo (ideally a ruler) is essential.

ANALYSING BIRD TRACKS

CONTEXT

Before getting too absorbed by the actual features of the track you've found, it is worth zooming out to a landscape level and refining your list of suspects that are likely in your location, the habitat you're in and the time of year. Many species are very specific in their preferences, and this may vary regionally and seasonally. For example, Curlew tracks are frequently encountered in upland areas and also can be found both on the coast and in fields. Where John grew up in north-east England, he frequently spotted Curlews on boggy farmland, not somewhere he expects to find them now in his adopted south coast county of Sussex. Many species are also migratory and may not even be in the country at the time you encounter a track. Bird tracking is no different to any form of tracking in that the more you know of the animals around you and their habits, the more accurate you will be with your identification and interpretation.

SUBSTRATE AND THE TRACK FLOOR

The medium that catches a track has a significant influence on the appearance of that track. Loose sand, for example, may blur the edges of a track, which in turn may make it look bigger than it really is. Conversely, the sand may also back-fill the track, making it look smaller than it really is. Substrates that allow the foot to sink deeply into the surface generally give the track a much bigger appearance than the foot that made it. Very hard substrates may make a track appear much more delicate than it really is and may not register all the track to the level of detail that would be most helpful.

All of this makes it important to find the true dimensions of the track floor. This is the point where the floor of the track stops and the walls of the substate the foot pushed through starts. This is true of anything that leaves a track in any substrate. Should a bird slide, then a toe may look longer than it really is, and the true track floor may need to be located carefully.

Tracks (like these Oystercatchers) can look totally different in different substrates.

The track floor of a Pheasant.

MORPHOLOGY

In mammal track identification the morphology of the track is much more important than the actual size. Large tracks of a species look like the small tracks of that same species. An adult Red Fox (*Vulpes vulpes*) track, for example, has the same features as a young Red Fox track, so size becomes useful only in general terms. Bird tracks are no exception to this but are slightly different to mammals in that (with a few exceptions, such as Ducks and Geese) by the time most species leave the nest their feet are adult-sized or very close to it. There are a number of features to look out for when analysing a bird track to determine what made it. When we talk about foot morphology, we are considering the features that are outlined in the sections below – Foot structure, Negative space, Toes and Toe pads, Nails, Angles and Size. Care has to be taken with similar adaptations or closely related species, again using Ducks and Geese as examples, where foot size and structure are very close in appearance. This is where we enter the realms of having to consider what may or may not be possible in species-level bird track recognition.

FOOT STRUCTURE

Birds are classified as digitigrade, which means they are standing on their equivalent of our human toes. Many bird species have an Anisodactyl foot structure of three toes pointing forwards and one – the Hallux – pointing backwards. In some instances, the backwards-facing Hallux is very much reduced or set high up the leg, or both, and therefore it may or may not show in the track. In a few species this toe is absent altogether, but in many it is long and shows reliably in the track. The Hallux, or Toe 1, is the equivalent of our human big toe. Bird toes are therefore numbered starting at the Hallux (Toe 1), and then numbered Toe 2, 3 and 4 from the inside towards the outside of the track. Birds do not have a Toe 5 or 'little toe'. Other toe arrangements do exist, including Zygodactyl (where Toes 2 and 3 point forwards and the Hallux and Toe 4 point backwards), and Syndactyl (where Toes 3 and 4 are fused along part of their length).

NEGATIVE SPACE

With all tracks – mammalian or avian – the negative space is the part of the track that isn't toes, nails or toe pads. In birds this is the Metatarsal area, the place in the middle of the foot where the Metatarsal bone (the bird's leg bone) is closest to the ground and where all the toes meet. It may be absent, large, or small and possibly forming patterns in the substrate if other parts of the foot influence the ground. In some species (and, indeed, groups of birds) it can be very distinctive and useful in identification. For example, many Gamebirds have a pad protecting the end of the Metatarsus that registers as a circular spot in the track.

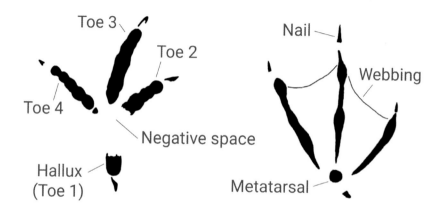

The elements of a bird track.

TOES AND TOE PADS

Toes form the main part of bird tracks and may be slender or robust, and this can often reflect their lifestyle. Birds that that walk as a preference generally have quite thick toes and robust looking feet – imagine a Pheasant or Chicken as familiar examples. Toe pads may also be slender or bulbous, and this is especially true of the pads on the ends of the Hallux and Toe 3. For a toe pad to be considered bulbous it would stick out beyond the line of the toe, not unlike the head of an unstruck match. Some birds may have bulbous pads in only one toe and perhaps not at the end if it has a specialised use such as clasping prey. In some cases, this feature alone may take you straight to the genus. Toes may be straight or, as in the case of Web-footed birds, often curve towards the centre of the track (which can be very helpful as the web does not always show in certain substrates). Some tracks may show a straight central toe (Toe 3), while with others it may curve or only curve towards the tip. These are all important features to consider when making an identification.

NAILS

Many species will register nails in their tracks that, as with toes and toe pads, can reflect their use. Applications as diverse as climbing up and down trees, holding food or scratching the ground require particular nail adaptations that can show as reliable features in the tracks of these birds. Some birds, Crows for example, have a larger nail on the end of their Hallux that is often dragged leaving a distinct trail. The Birds of Prey are perhaps the most highly adapted with their nails having evolved into long, robust claws (or talons) for holding and killing their prey.

ANGLES

The angles that the toes leave the Metatarsal area may be useful when considering Toes 2 and 4, and their relationship to Toe 3, the central toe. These may be symmetrical to Toe 3, held out wide, or close (resulting in a narrow track). It could be that one toe sits closer to Toe 3 than another. We have noticed in studying tracks in some detail that birds move their toes, and they do so quite significantly. In one trail of an individual Green Sandpiper there was 30 per cent variation in the toe angles. For this reason, we felt that putting an empirical measurement on the angles would be misleading, and rather we would like to encourage you to notice the overall impression of the angles.

MEASURING BIRD TRACKS

We have included measurements for the species described. We do not include nails in these measurements as often they do not show in the tracks. For track length, birds with an absent or reduced Hallux (e.g., Gamebirds and Waders) are measured from the back of the Metatarsal area to the tip of the leading Toe 3. Classic bird tracks are measured from the end of the toe pads on Toe 3 to the end of the toe pad on the Hallux. The Zygodactyl bird tracks are measured from the end of Toe 3 to the end of Toe 4 (in Woodpeckers), the Hallux to Toe 2 (in Owls), and also the Totipalmate tracks from the end of the Hallux to the end of Toe 4. When measuring tracks of the same individual within a trail, we have found up to 10 per cent variation in our measurements, and up to 20 per cent variation in length (on average) between individuals of the same species (this being even greater where the species are significantly sexually dimorphic). So, keep this variation in mind when attempting to measure and identify the bird tracks you find. We have decided not to include width measurements, having found through researching this book that birds are able to change the width of their tracks (see *Angles* above) quite considerably, to a point that width measurement becomes unreliable. Below are the (left) track silhouettes of a Robin, Pheasant, Tawny Owl, Green Woodpecker and Cormorant showing how we have measured Classic, Gamebird, Zygodactyl (two types) and Totipalmate tracks.

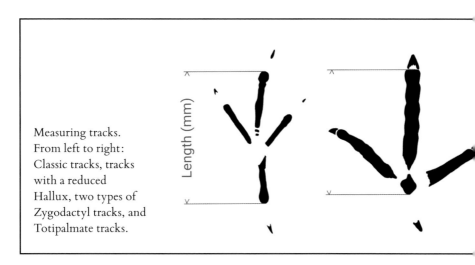

Measuring tracks. From left to right: Classic tracks, tracks with a reduced Hallux, two types of Zygodactyl tracks, and Totipalmate tracks.

GAITS AND TRACK PATTERNS

We describe gaits as the way a mammal or bird is moving. In the case of birds, they will walk, hop, run and skip. We describe the track pattern as the sequence of tracks the bird leaves on the ground when moving in a specific gait. Compared to mammals, birds tend to be a little easier when it comes to working out how they are moving as there are only two instead of four limbs to worry about! Noting the pattern can be a useful aid to identification. Birds tend to be relatively predictable (and unchanging) with their gait. It would be unusual, for example, to see a Partridge hopping; they tend to walk or run. Finches tend to hop everywhere, and Wood Pigeons walk. It would be unusual to find any of these birds doing anything other than their normal gait. If a bird comes out of its normal or baseline gait it normally doesn't stay in that gait for very long. Studying the track pattern can often get you to a general group, so it is a useful aid in identification. Think about the birds you see regularly in the garden, and imagine the way they move and how that may look as a trail.

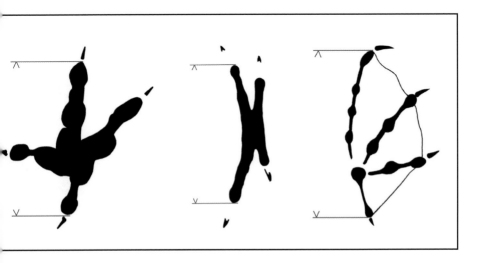

When working out track patterns, we need a few pieces of terminology in place:

Stride: A stride is the distance between the track made by one foot, to the point that same foot is seen again. The half stride is the point between the foot on one side of the body (let's say the left foot) to that on the other side (in this case, the right foot).

Straddle: The straddle is described as the width of the trail the bird leaves, and represents the distance between the outer edges of the tracks – the outside edge of the left foot to the edge of the right foot. Like the stride, this is also useful in determining walks from runs but also gives an indication of the size of the bird in walks and the hopping and skipping gaits.

Walks and runs: Walks show a short stride and a (relatively) wide straddle. When the same bird speeds up into a run, the straddle narrows and the stride lengthens.

Hops: Hops show as paired, parallel tracks and is a gait employed by many birds such as the Finches and Sparrows, Dunnock, Robin, Woodpeckers and Jay. Thrushes will also often hop.

Skips: Like hops, skips also involve the feet being paired but, unlike hops, the feet hit the ground at slightly different times and leave trails with one track of the pair in front of the other. To find a great example of mixing gaits, watch a Blackbird in good substrate. Blackbirds often hop, run, stop and then hop or run again. This leaves a trail of paired tracks, then a long stride, narrow straddle pattern, then a stop, paired or nearly paired tracks, and then the run again. The Crows frequently add skips into their walking trails (as they speed up), as do Snow Buntings.

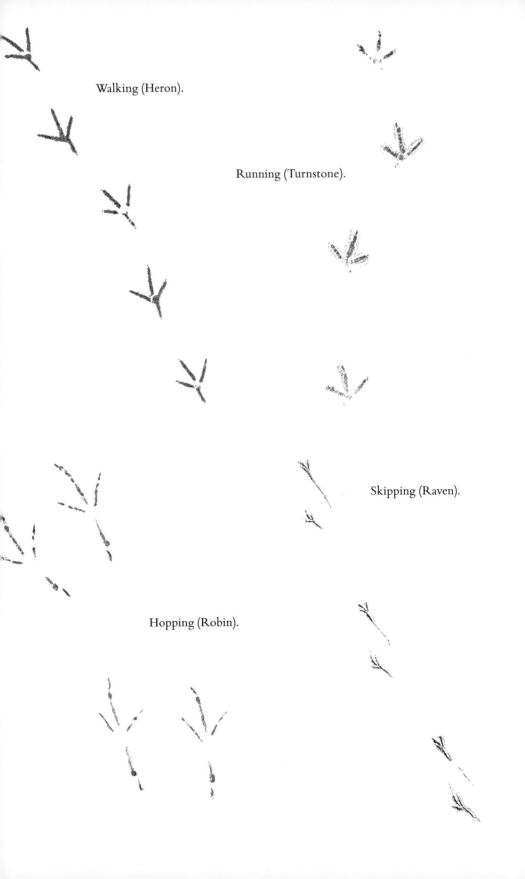

Walking (Heron).

Running (Turnstone).

Skipping (Raven).

Hopping (Robin).

USING THIS BOOK

This book covers 138 species that we have found over a three-year period around the British Isles and in mainland Europe. Many are found commonly, but some we have found only once or twice. We have also sourced track photos from the tracking community for those species that we know often leave tracks but which we have been unable to find ourselves.

The 138 species have been grouped by their foot morphology and track structure, and therefore the sequence will seem a little unfamiliar if you are used to referencing bird field guides that tend to be organised taxonomically. So, the species are grouped into broad sections (such as *Classic bird tracks*), with an introduction to the general track type and characteristics of that group. Some of these broad groups have been further divided based on a specific feature or relationship (e.g., into Crows, or Pigeons and Doves), each with a detailed explanation that's then followed by the individual species descriptions. These species descriptions include line drawings of the track, sometimes the trail they leave, and a selection of photographs of the species' tracks. The species are broadly ordered by size (largest first), but with some variation to keep the most similar-looking tracks together.

In the following section – *Bird tracks of the British Isles: life-sized drawings* – are the tracks for all 138 bird species in this book, in the order and groupings they can be found in within the book (and with page number references to take you to the relevant section for that track type). Except where noted on the tracks of some of our largest birds, the tracks in this book are all life-sized (the trails are not), and where there is just one track illustrated it will always be of the left foot.

THE BIRD TRACKS JOURNEY

It is almost inevitable that we will stumble across (or be sent) the tracks of a new species as soon as this book is published, and that's the nature of tracking and learning about the wildlife around us – it is an endless and exciting journey of discovery that we hope this book will inspire you to make and help you to navigate. If you discover tracks that aren't in this book, please do share them so that we can all learn. And if you are indeed inspired to investigate wildlife tracking more generally, please visit www.europeanwildlifetracking.com, take a look at our Instagram feeds and consider getting John's more general book *Track and Sign: A Guide to the Field Signs of Mammals and Birds of the UK* (2021, also published by The History Press). www.woodcraftschool.co.uk/books.

BIRD TRACKS OF THE BRITISH ISLES: LIFE-SIZED DRAWINGS

SMALL PASSERINES (see pages 86–123)

Blackbird
Turdus merula.

Song Thrush
Turdus philomelos.

Starling
Sturnus vulgaris.

Robin
Erithacus rubecula.

Great Tit
Parus major.

Blue Tit
Cyanistes caeruleus.

Nuthatch
Sitta europaea.

Blackcap
Sylvia atricapilla.

Chaffinch
Fringilla coelebs.

Linnet
Linaria cannabina.

Twite
Linaria flavirostris.

Goldfinch
Carduelis carduelis.

House Sparrow
Passer domesticus.

Snow Bunting
Plectrophenax nivalis.

Reed Bunting
Emberiza schoeniclus.

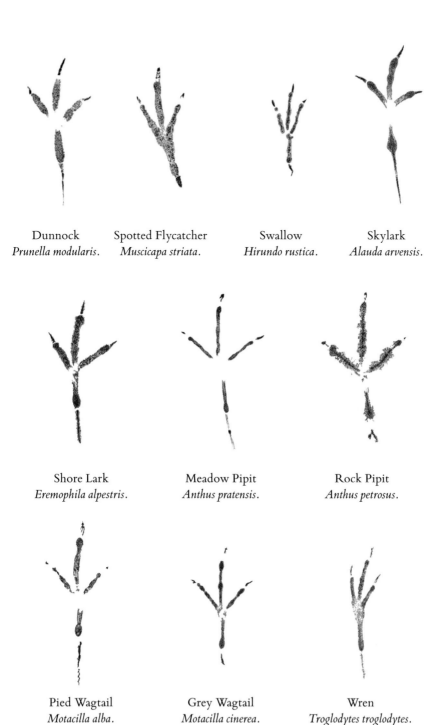

Dunnock
Prunella modularis.

Spotted Flycatcher
Muscicapa striata.

Swallow
Hirundo rustica.

Skylark
Alauda arvensis.

Shore Lark
Eremophila alpestris.

Meadow Pipit
Anthus pratensis.

Rock Pipit
Anthus petrosus.

Pied Wagtail
Motacilla alba.

Grey Wagtail
Motacilla cinerea.

Wren
Troglodytes troglodytes.

SYNDACTYL (see page 124)

Common Kingfisher
Alcedo atthis.

PIGEONS AND DOVES (see pages 126–132)

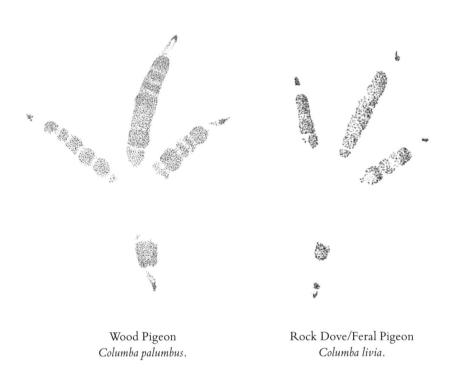

Wood Pigeon
Columba palumbus.

Rock Dove/Feral Pigeon
Columba livia.

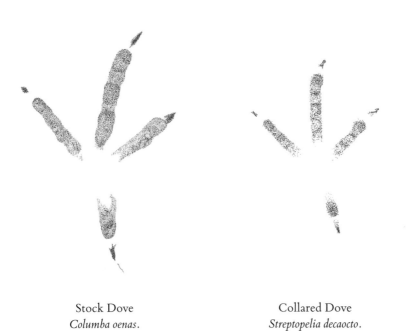

Stock Dove
Columba oenas.

Collared Dove
Streptopelia decaocto.

Turtle Dove
Streptopelia turtur.

CROWS (see pages 133–147)

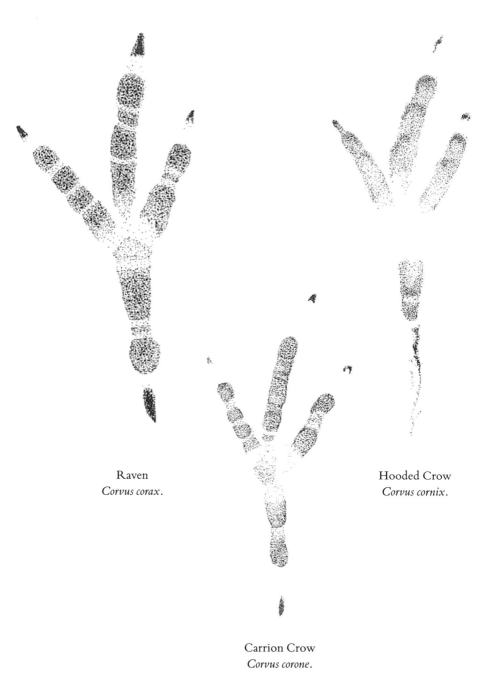

Raven
Corvus corax.

Hooded Crow
Corvus cornix.

Carrion Crow
Corvus corone.

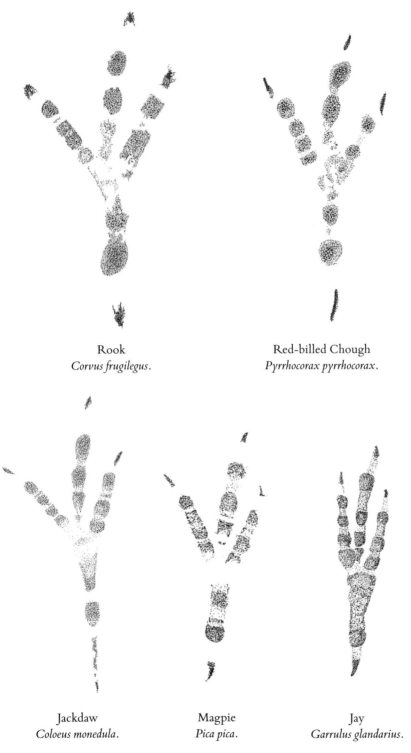

Rook
Corvus frugilegus.

Red-billed Chough
Pyrrhocorax pyrrhocorax.

Jackdaw
Coloeus monedula.

Magpie
Pica pica.

Jay
Garrulus glandarius.

BIRDS OF PREY (see pages 148–167)

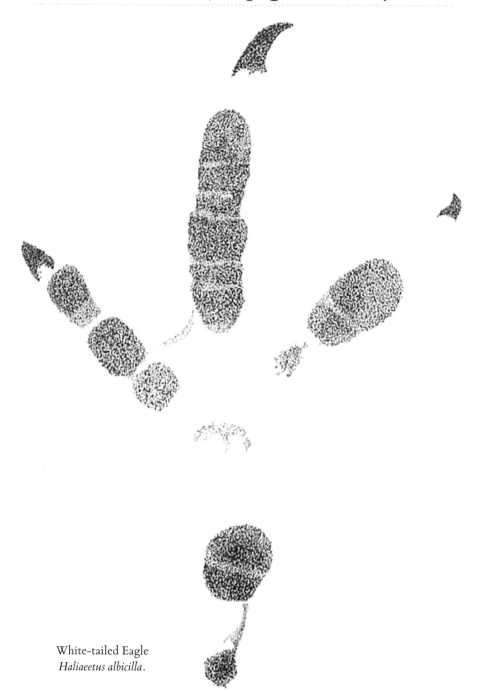

White-tailed Eagle
Haliaeetus albicilla.

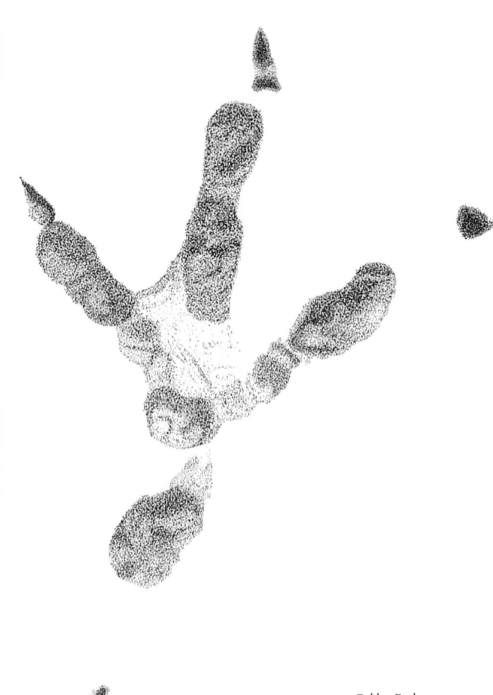

Golden Eagle
Aquila chrysaetos.

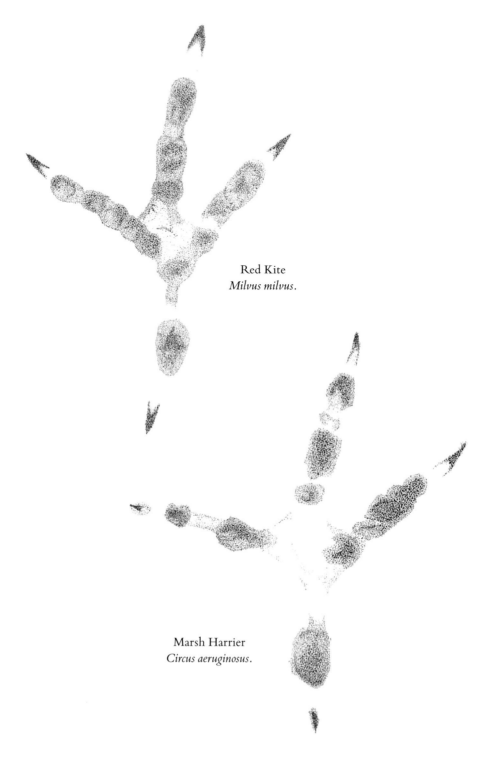

Red Kite
Milvus milvus.

Marsh Harrier
Circus aeruginosus.

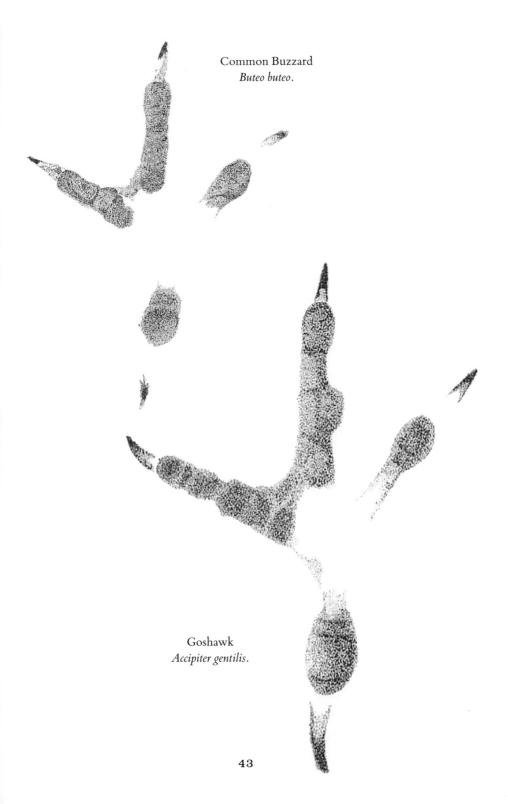

Common Buzzard
Buteo buteo.

Goshawk
Accipiter gentilis.

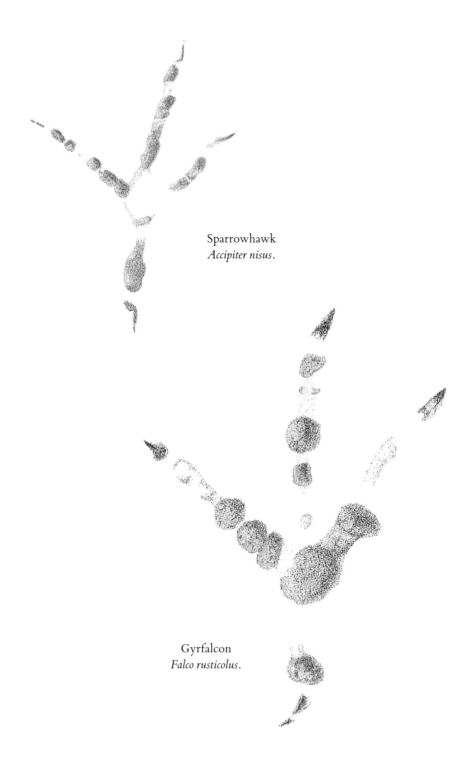

Sparrowhawk
Accipiter nisus.

Gyrfalcon
Falco rusticolus.

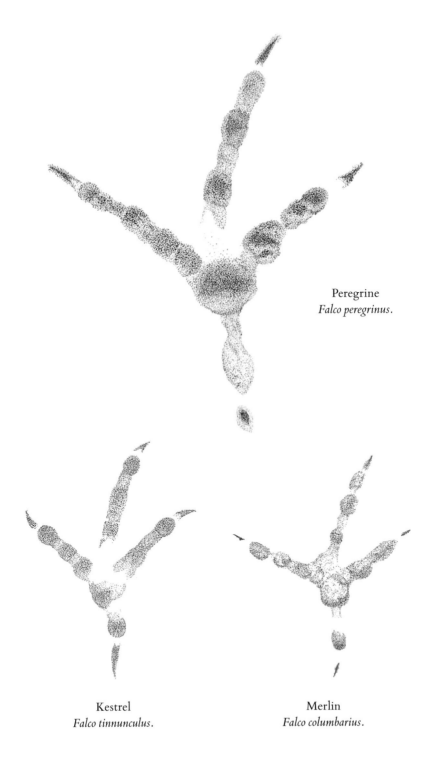

Peregrine
Falco peregrinus.

Kestrel
Falco tinnunculus.

Merlin
Falco columbarius.

OWLS (see pages 169–180)

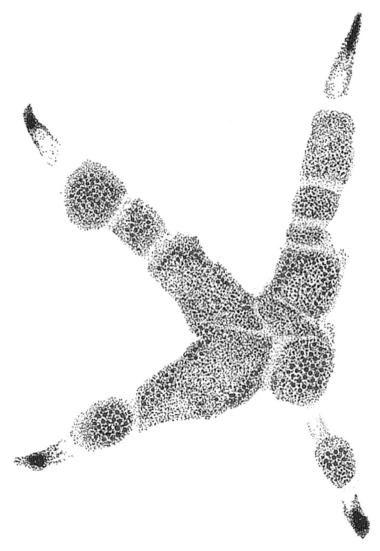

Eurasian Eagle-Owl
Bubo bubo.

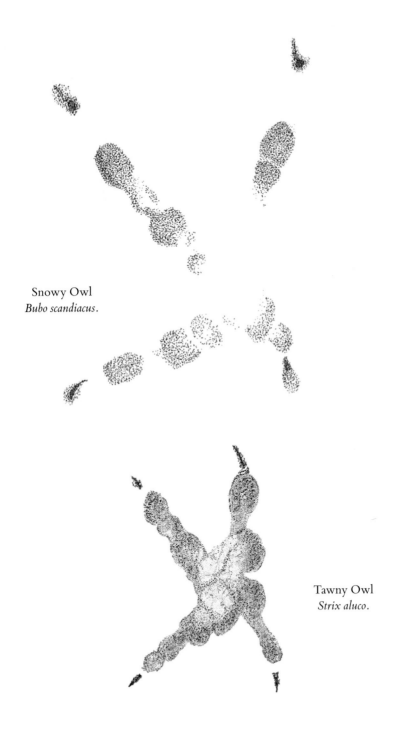

Snowy Owl
Bubo scandiacus.

Tawny Owl
Strix aluco.

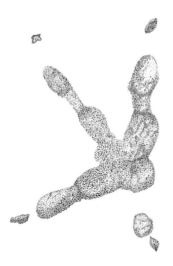

Short-eared Owl
Asio flammeus.

Long-eared Owl
Asio otus.

Barn Owl
Tyto alba.

Little Owl
Athene Noctua.

WOODPECKERS AND PARAKEETS

(see pages 181–185)

Green Woodpecker
Picus viridis.

Great Spotted Woodpecker
Dendrocopos major.

Rose-ringed Parakeet
Psittacula krameria.

GAMEBIRDS (see pages 187–208)

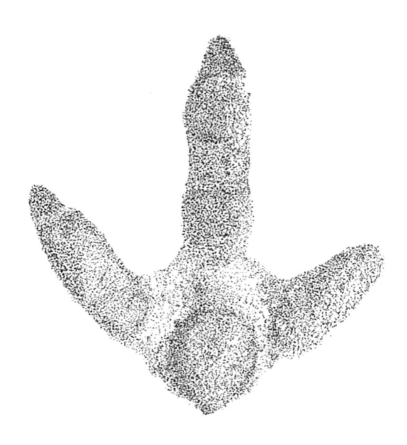

Great Bustard
Otis tarda.

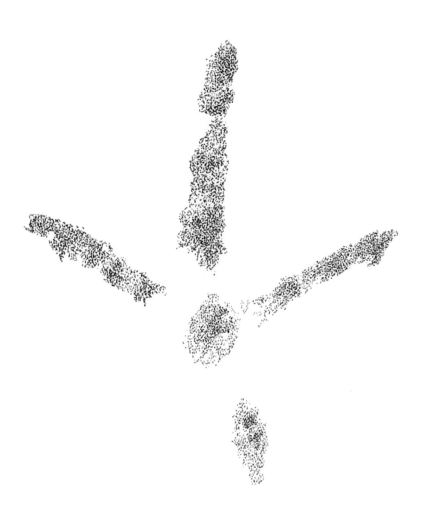

Capercaillie
Tetrao urogallus.

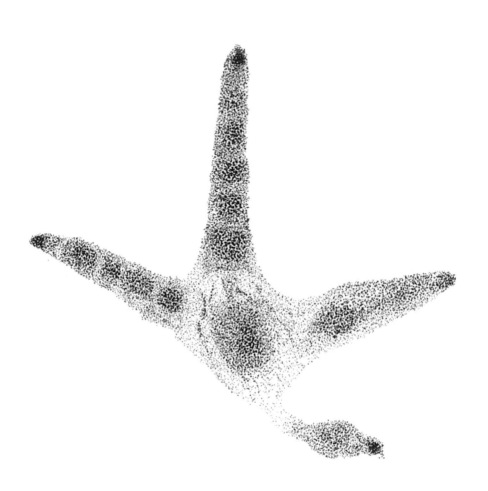

Domestic Turkey
Meleagris gallopavo domesticus.

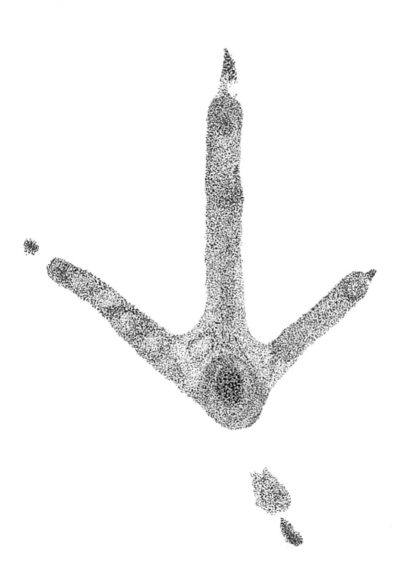

Indian Peafowl (Peacock)
Pavo cristatus.

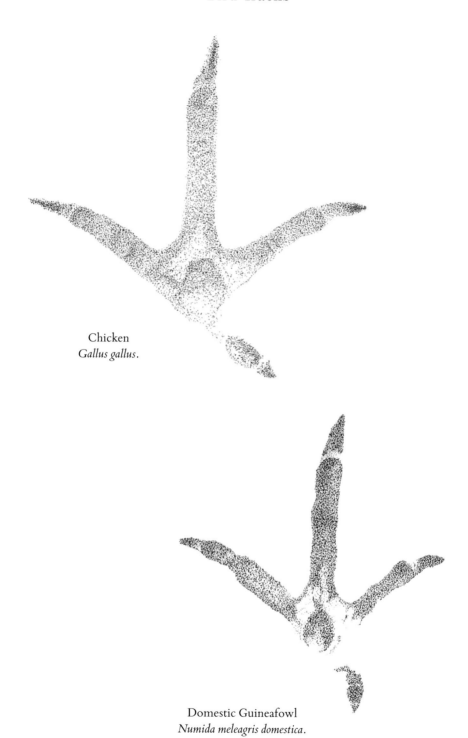

Chicken
Gallus gallus.

Domestic Guineafowl
Numida meleagris domestica.

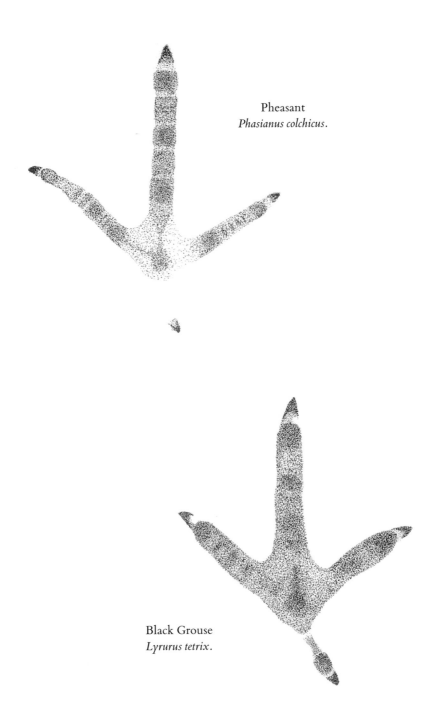

Pheasant
Phasianus colchicus.

Black Grouse
Lyrurus tetrix.

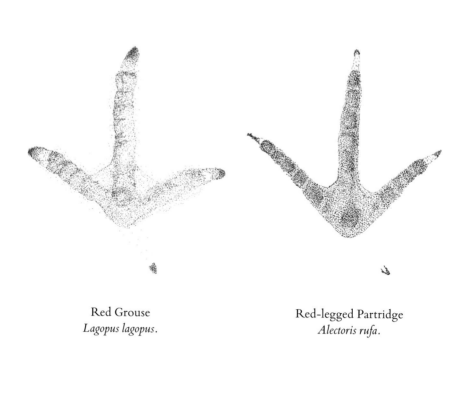

Red Grouse
Lagopus lagopus.

Red-legged Partridge
Alectoris rufa.

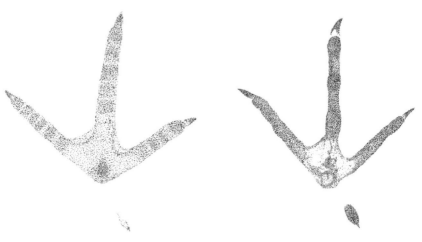

Grey Partridge
Perdix perdix.

Common Quail
Coturnix coturnix.

WADERS (see pages 209–245)

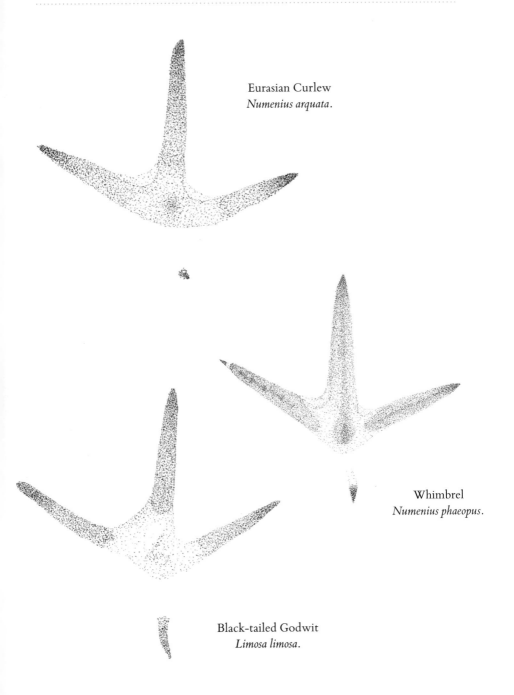

Eurasian Curlew
Numenius arquata.

Whimbrel
Numenius phaeopus.

Black-tailed Godwit
Limosa limosa.

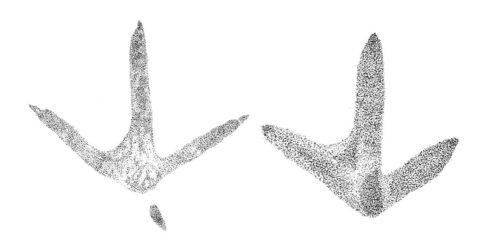

Bar-tailed Godwit
Limosa lapponica.

Oystercatcher
Haematopus ostralegus.

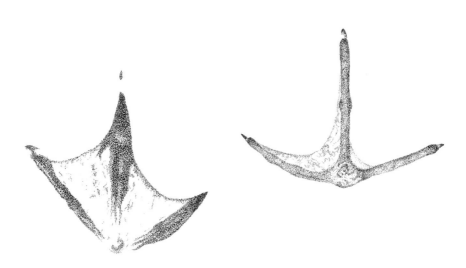

Pied Avocet
Recurvirostra avosetta.

Black-winged Stilt
Himantopus Himantopus.

Bird Tracks of the British Isles: Life-Sized Drawings

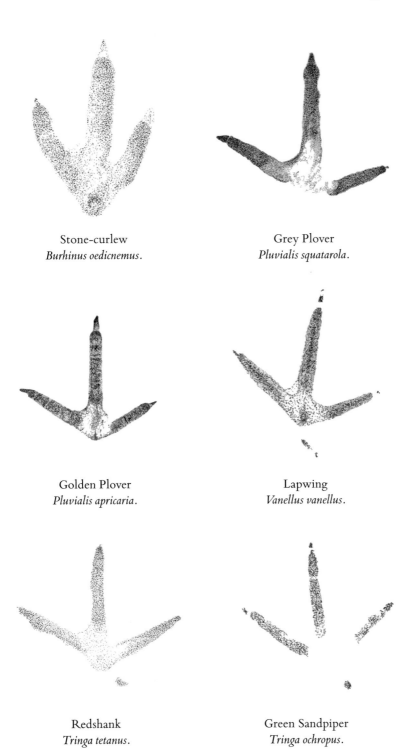

Stone-curlew
Burhinus oedicnemus.

Grey Plover
Pluvialis squatarola.

Golden Plover
Pluvialis apricaria.

Lapwing
Vanellus vanellus.

Redshank
Tringa tetanus.

Green Sandpiper
Tringa ochropus.

Turnstone
Arenaria interpres.

Common Sandpiper
Actitis hypoleucos.

Ringed Plover
Charadrius hiaticula.

Dunlin
Calidris alpina.

Little Ringed Plover
Charadrius dubius.

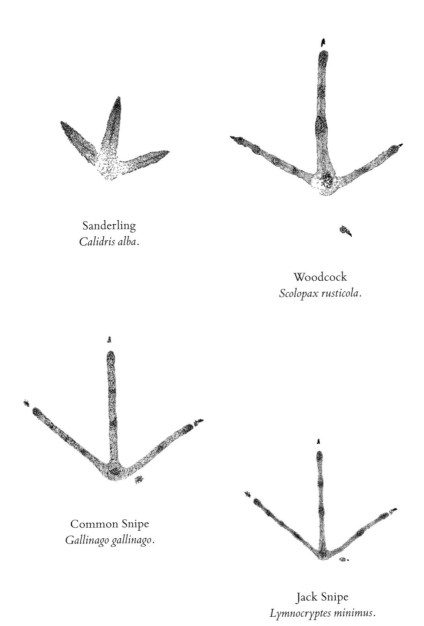

Sanderling
Calidris alba.

Woodcock
Scolopax rusticola.

Common Snipe
Gallinago gallinago.

Jack Snipe
Lymnocryptes minimus.

WATER BIRDS (see pages 247–266)

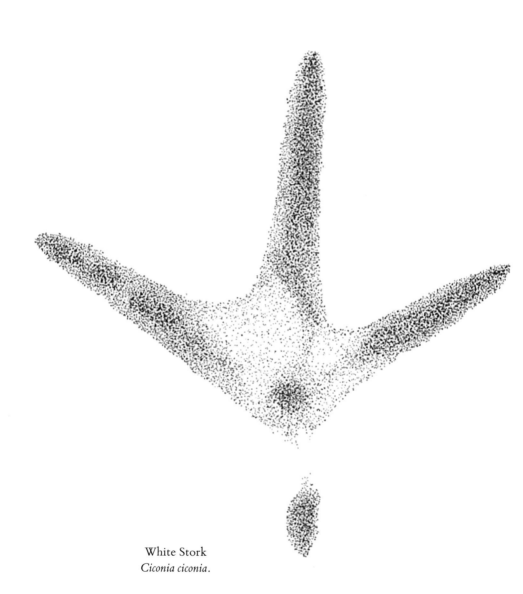

White Stork
Ciconia ciconia.

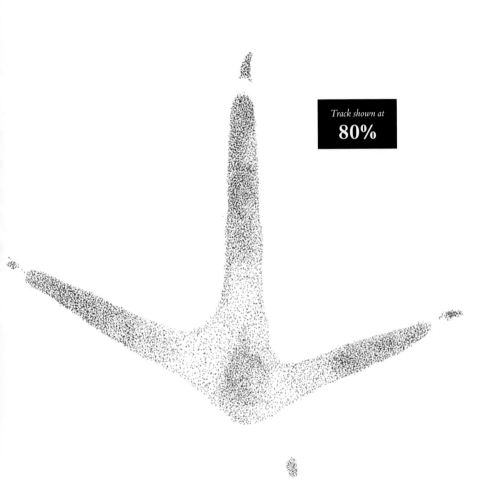

Track shown at
80%

Common Crane
Grus grus.

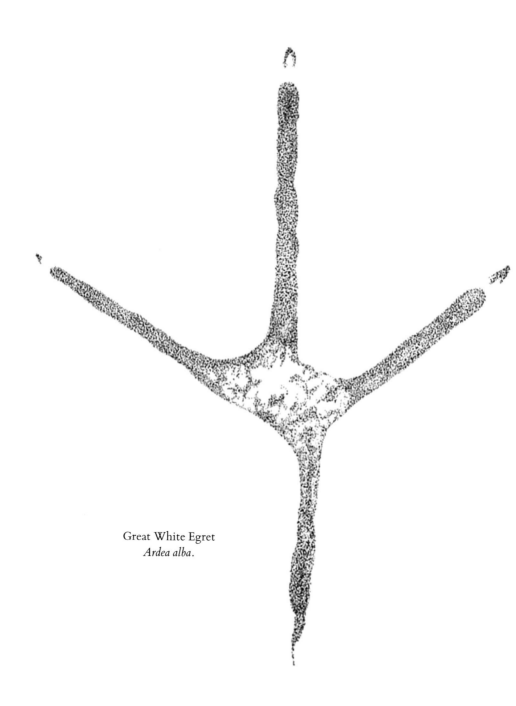

Great White Egret
Ardea alba.

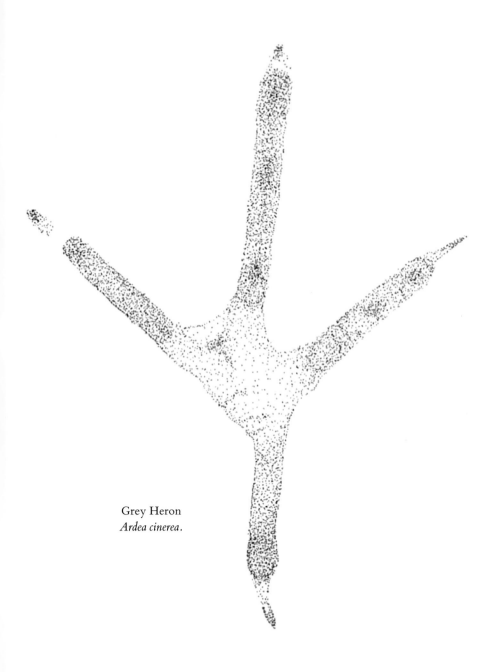

Grey Heron
Ardea cinerea.

Bird Tracks

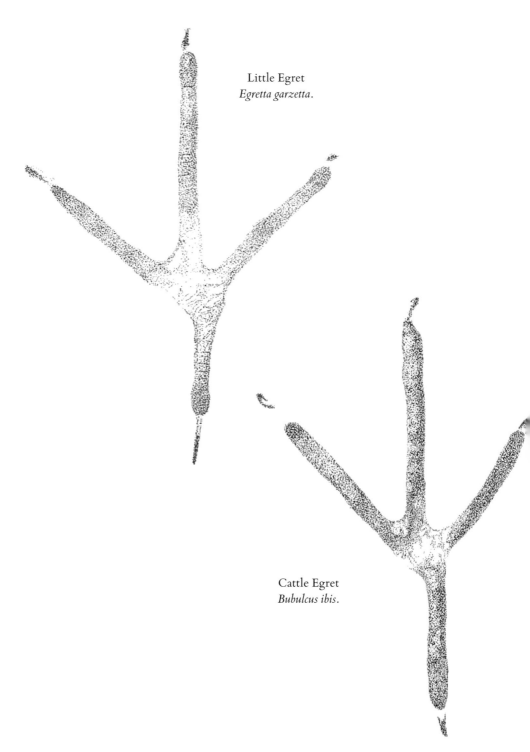

Little Egret
Egretta garzetta.

Cattle Egret
Bubulcus ibis.

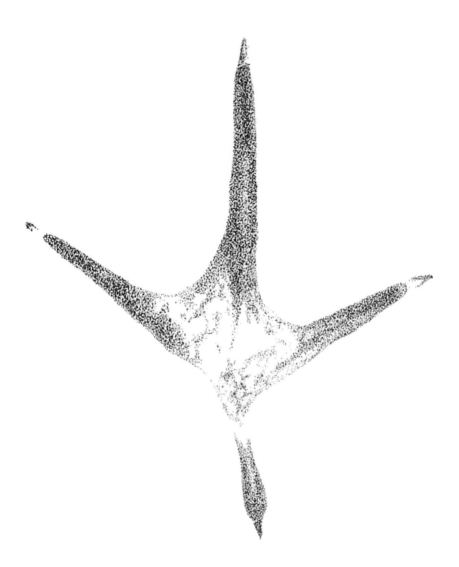

Spoonbill
Platalea leucorodia.

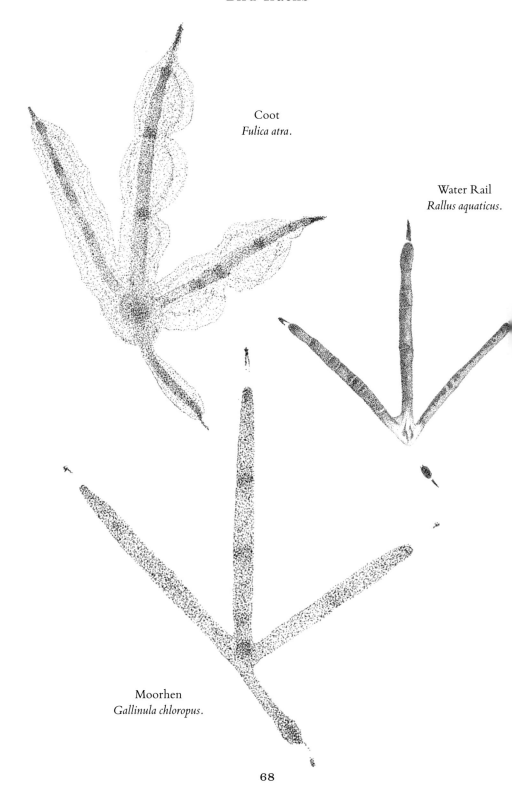

Coot
Fulica atra.

Water Rail
Rallus aquaticus.

Moorhen
Gallinula chloropus.

SWANS, GEESE AND DUCKS

(see pages 268–304)

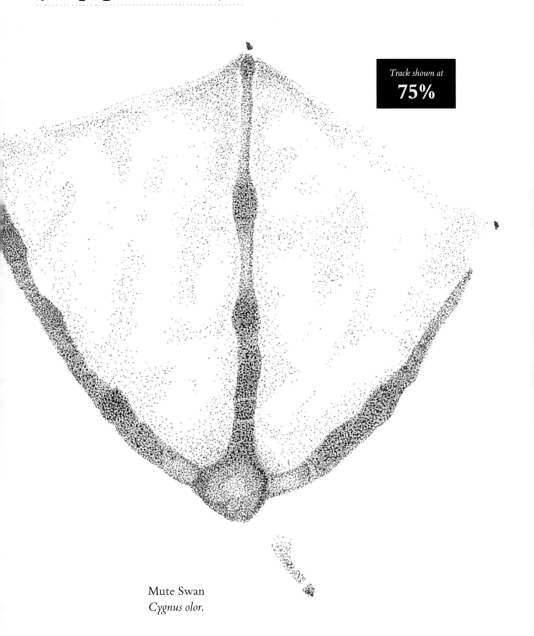

Track shown at
75%

Mute Swan
Cygnus olor.

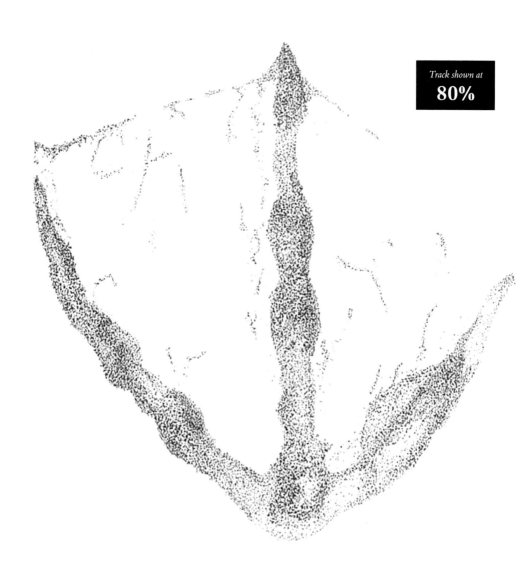

Track shown at
80%

Whooper Swan
Cygnus cygnus.

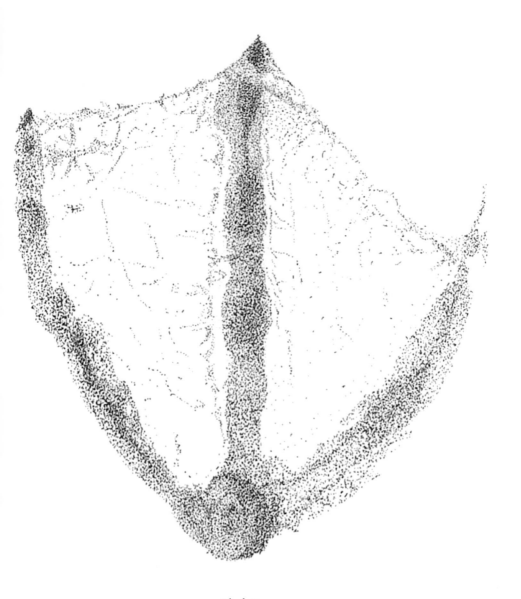

Black Swan
Cygnus atratus.

Canada Goose
Branta canadensis.

Greylag Goose
Anser anser.

White-fronted Goose
Anser albifrons.

Pink-footed Goose
Anser brachyrhynchus.

Egyptian Goose
Alopochen aegyptiaca.

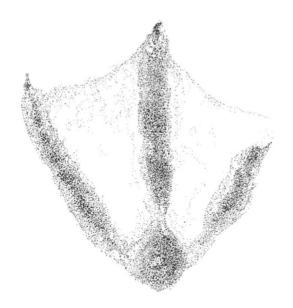

Barnacle Goose
Branta leucopsis.

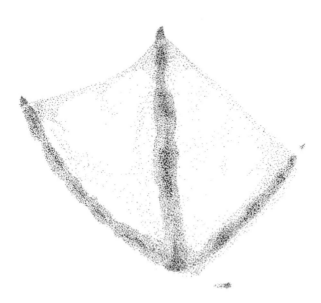

Brent Goose
Branta bernicla.

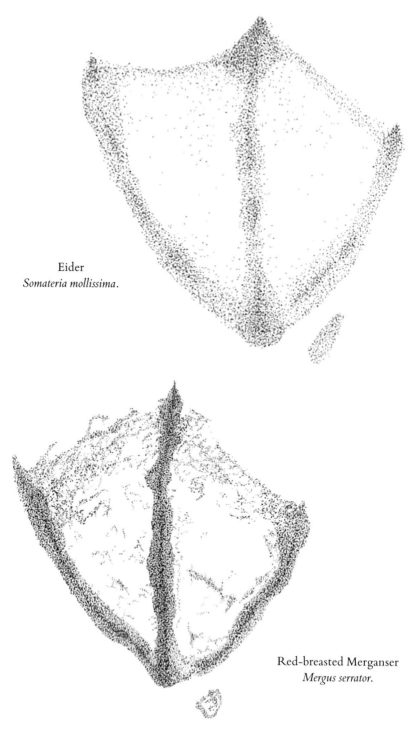

Eider
Somateria mollissima.

Red-breasted Merganser
Mergus serrator.

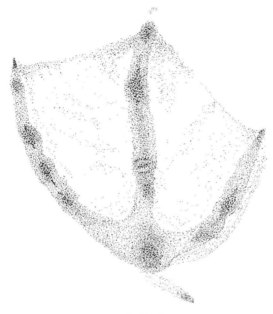

Shelduck
Tadorna tadorna.

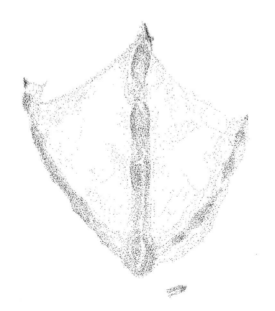

Mallard
Anas platyrhynchos.

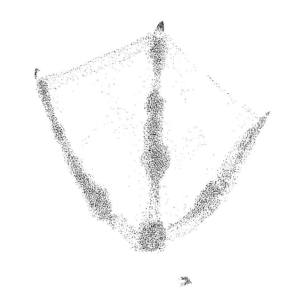

Pintail
Anas acuta.

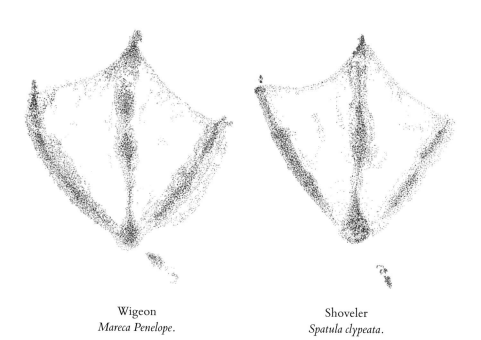

Wigeon
Mareca Penelope.

Shoveler
Spatula clypeata.

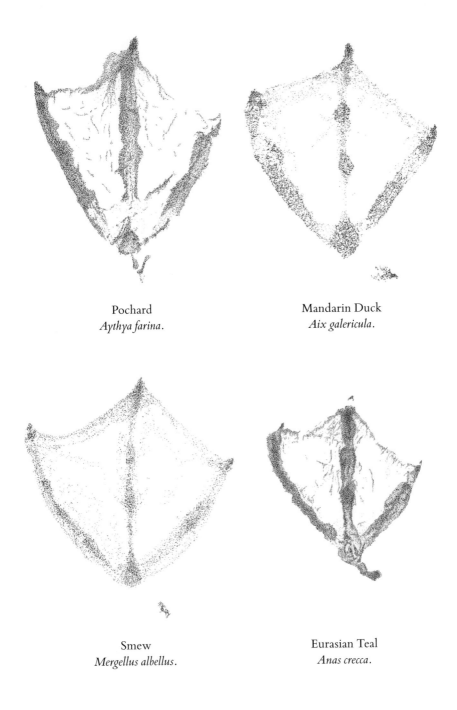

Pochard
Aythya farina.

Mandarin Duck
Aix galericula.

Smew
Mergellus albellus.

Eurasian Teal
Anas crecca.

GULLS AND TERNS (see pages 305–322)

Arctic Skua
Stercorarius parasiticus.

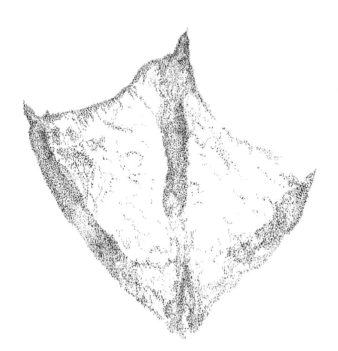

Great Black-backed Gull
Larus marinus.

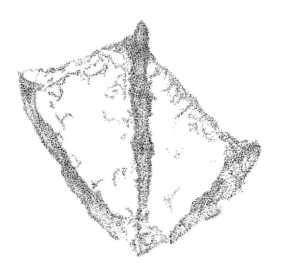

Lesser Black-backed Gull
Larus fuscus.

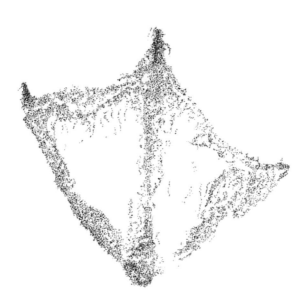

Herring Gull
Larus argentatus.

Bird Tracks

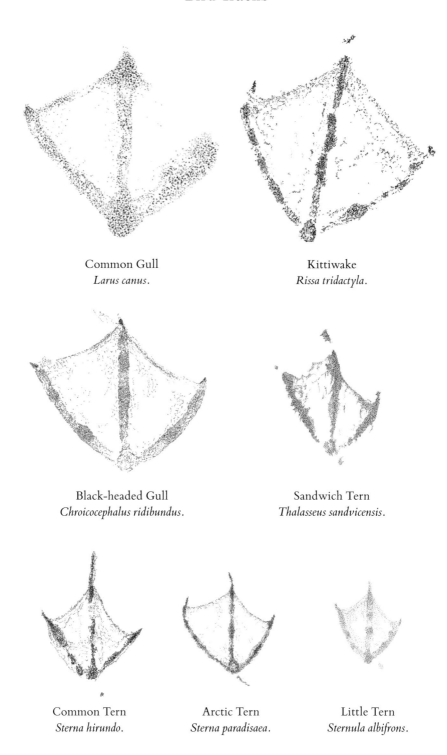

Common Gull
Larus canus.

Kittiwake
Rissa tridactyla.

Black-headed Gull
Chroicocephalus ridibundus.

Sandwich Tern
Thalasseus sandvicensis.

Common Tern
Sterna hirundo.

Arctic Tern
Sterna paradisaea.

Little Tern
Sternula albifrons.

TOTIPALMATE (see pages 323–328)

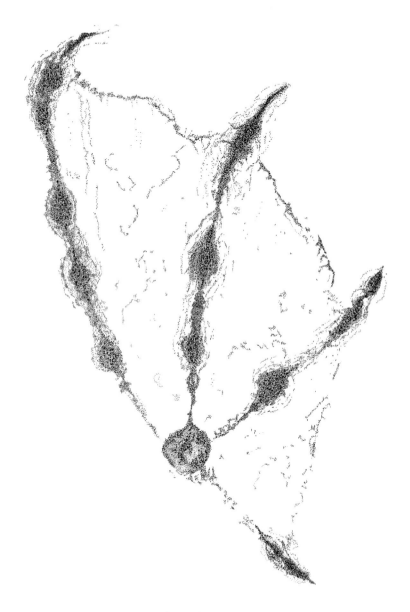

Great Cormorant
Phalacrocorax carobo.

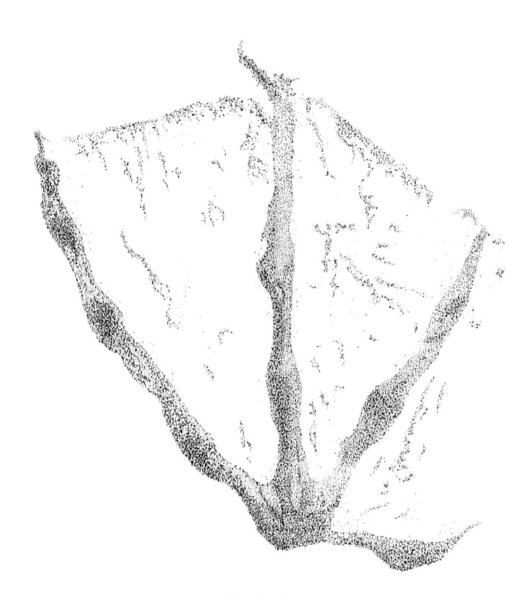

Northern Gannet
Morus bassanus.

CLASSIC BIRD TRACKS

Should a child be asked to draw a bird track, it is likely that their track would have three toes facing forwards and one back. This 'classic' track is properly termed Anisodactyl, with the three toes – Toes 2, 3 and 4 – facing forwards. The shorter of the outer toes is Toe 2 if there is a difference. The Hallux or Toe 1, our big toe equivalent, is facing back.

These classic bird feet belong, among others, to our Passerines – the perching birds or song birds. Imagine these birds sitting on a branch with the Hallux wrapping under and around that branch to keep them from falling off. There are many species in this group with this foot structure. These include Pigeons, Crows and Birds of Prey, as well as the water birds, many of which are described in this book.

SMALL PASSERINES

Small Passerines all show classic bird tracks that may show variations in toe angle, toe pads or symmetry. The species described below are grouped based on similar characteristics.

THRUSHES AND THRUSH-LIKE PASSERINE TRACKS

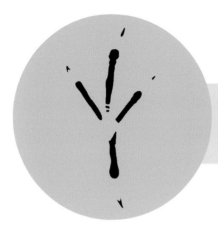

Track type: Classic.
Track size: Small (26–40mm).
Key features: Bulbous toe pads.

SPECIES

Blackbird *Turdus merula*   Song Thrush *Turdus philomelos*
Starling *Sturnus vulgaris*   Robin *Erithacus rubecula*

There are several species that show bulbous toe pads at the end of the Hallux (Toe 1), Toe 3, or both. The most commonly encountered are those of the Thrush genus *Turdus*. We describe bulbous toe pads as being 'matchstick-like', with the toe pad resembling the head of the match, and the toe being the stick. The Thrush family shows this reliably on Toe 3 and also on the Hallux (Toe 1). We have not had a chance to examine the tracks of the other British members of this group (namely Fieldfare, Redwing and Mistle Thrush), but as far as we can ascertain these all have the same characteristics. Indeed, looking further afield it seems that all *Turdus* species may be similar, and certainly the American Robin (*T. migratorius*), which we have studied, shows these same features.

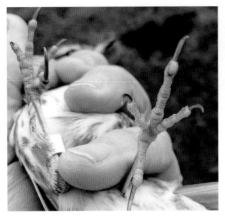

The feet of Redwing (left) and Fieldfare (right).

Similar-sized species in this group may be very difficult if not impossible to separate in the field. Most confusable with the Thrushes are Starlings, for which reason we include a description for this bird in this section. We also include Robin here as its tracks resemble a small, slender Blackbird or even Starling. All tend towards a curving (or bent) end to Toe 3. If the characteristic bulbous toe of the *Turdus* is not present or obvious, they are easily confused. Look for Starlings leaving multiple tracks – as they are social, flocking creatures it is really quite unusual to find just single tracks (at least in good substrates, that is). Both Blackbird and Song Thrush tracks are found commonly, and are often the first small bird tracks that a new bird track enthusiast will encounter. Song Thrushes have a tendency for the outer toes to curve down at the tips, and the leading toe (Toe 3) is curved into the centre of the trail. Blackbird tracks also have this toe pointing towards the centre of the trail but the digit itself tends to be straight.

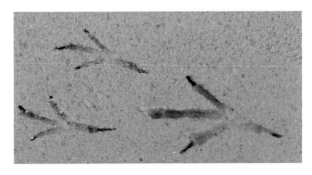

Note the similarities in morphology of the smaller Robin tracks and the Blackbird track on the right.

TITS AND TIT-LIKE PASSERINE TRACKS

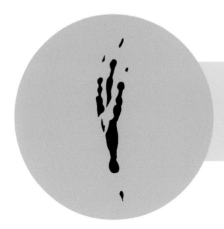

Track type: Classic.
Track size: Small (18–28mm).
Key features: Hugging outer and inner toes.

SPECIES

Great Tit *Parus major*   Blue Tit *Cyanistes caeruleus*
Nuthatch *Sitta europaea*   Blackcap *Sylvia atricapilla*

Hugging toes are found with a number of small birds in the British Isles and resemble miniature Jay tracks. Toe 3 is central and straight and the forward-facing Toes 2 and 4 are held very close to it, effectively hugging it. The Hallux is long and obvious. Characteristic birds in this category include the Nuthatch and the Tits. We have studied the tracks of Great Tit and Blue Tit, and it seems (through studying birds in the hand) that the other Tits (Coal Tit, Marsh Tit and Long-Tailed Tit, at least) have the same foot structure. We have included Blackcap here having found their tracks to be very similar, and it's likely that the other *Sylvia* Warblers will be, too. We speculate that this toe arrangement is an adaptation for life in the trees.

FINCHES AND FINCH-LIKE PASSERINE TRACKS

Track type: Classic.
Track size: Small (20–27mm).
Key features: Hallux and Toe 3 curve towards the centre of the trail.

SPECIES

Chaffinch *Fringilla coelebs*
Twite *Linaria flavirostris*
House Sparrow *Passer domesticus*
Snow Bunting *Plectrophenax nivalis*
Spotted Flycatcher *Muscicapa striata*

Linnet *Linaria cannabina*
Goldfinch *Carduelis carduelis*
Reed Bunting *Emberiza schoeniclus*
Dunnock *Prunella modularis*

We have found Finches to be really quite tricky to separate and it is likely that the tracker would need to rely heavily on relative size, and habitat context. Otherwise, similar-sized Finches are, in our opinion, inseparable from each other. Classically, Finch tracks curve from the Hallux through Toe 3 towards the centre of the trail, effectively making them pigeon-toed. They register the Metatarsal area quite weakly. Toes 2 and 4 describe quite acute angles in relation to the leading Toe 3, and in most cases the tracks are symmetrical. Although we were unable to study every Finch species, it is very likely that they will have very similar structure and therefore tracks. We have also included the Buntings, House Sparrow and Dunnock in this section as they are very similar in foot structure to Finches.

SWALLOW AND MARTIN TRACKS

Track type: Classic.
Track size: Small (19mm).
Key features: Short Hallux.

SPECIES

Swallow *Hirundo rustica*

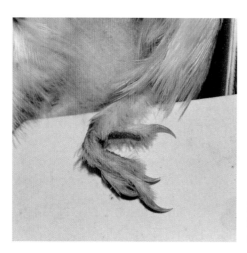

House Martin feet from a museum specimen. (HVG)

We have only been able to include one representative in this category – the Swallow – although both House and Sand Martins have a very similar foot structure and will probably leave very similar tracks. Their tracks are only likely to be found where adults are collecting mud for nest building in the breeding season, and are likely to be associated with beak marks in the mud.

House Martins collecting mud for nest building. (ID)

LARKS, PIPITS AND WAGTAIL TRACKS

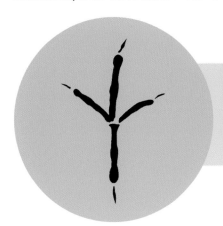

Track type: Classic.
Track size: Small (23–30mm).
Key features: Long Hallux and
Hallux nail.

SPECIES

Skylark *Alauda arvensis*
Rock Pipit *Anthus petrosus*
Pied Wagtail *Motacilla alba*
Wren *Troglodytes troglodytes*

Shore Lark *Eremophila alpestris*
Meadow Pipit *Anthus pratensis*
Grey Wagtail *Motacilla cinerea*

This group is characterised by having an obvious long nail on the Hallux (and, indeed, a long Hallux). In the case of the Pipits and Wagtails, this long Hallux nail often leaves drag marks in the trail and shows reliably in the tracks. The Larks show the addition of quite bulbous toe pads, and the Wagtails have two toes quite obviously offset. The Wren is in this group because of its proportionately long Hallux and nail, but tends to hop.

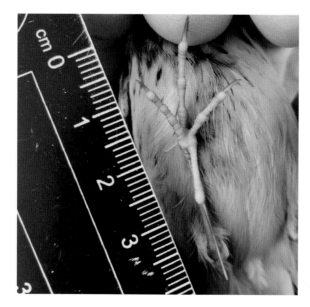

Meadow Pipit foot showing its long Hallux nail.

SMALL PASSERINES TRACK DESCRIPTIONS

BLACKBIRD (*TURDUS MERULA*)

Track: 40mm. Classic bird track comprising slender, elegant toes with prominent toe pads at the end of the Hallux and especially Toe 3. The overall track appears obviously curved, with Toe 3 angled towards the centre of the trail (although the toe itself is straight). The Metatarsal area rarely registers (leaving a large negative space in the track). Toe 4 often presents at a greater angle than the inner Toe 2, although angles can be quite variable. Blackbirds tend to skip and hop (and occasionally run) and the resulting track pattern can help in identification.

Similar Species: Other Thrushes have similar tracks (see Song Thrush) but vary subtly in terms of size and proportions. Starling tracks are very similar but with more robust toes, less obvious bulbous toe ends and a proportionately shorter Hallux. Toes 2 and 4 in Starling tracks tend to be held closer to Toe 3 than in Blackbird, but this is not reliable.

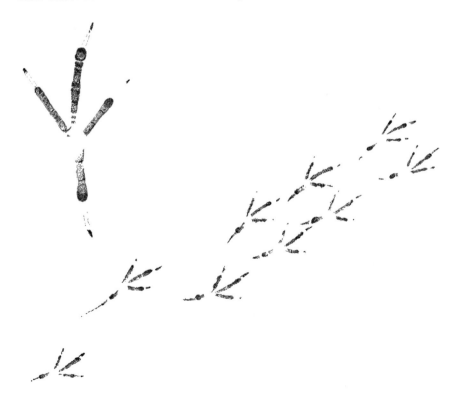

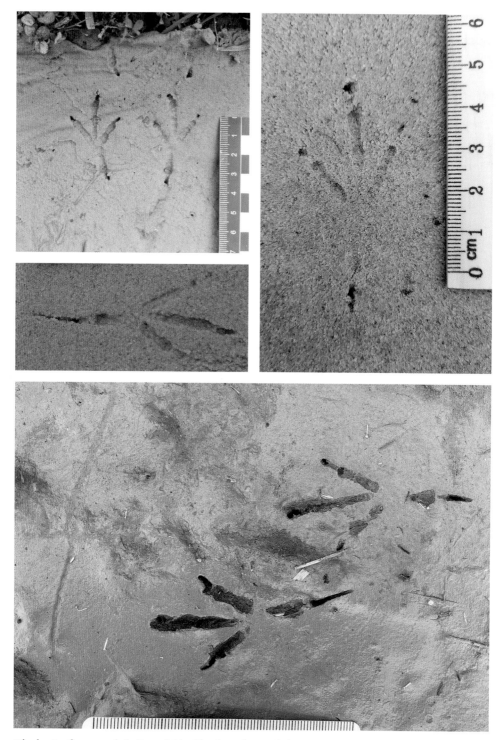

Clockwise from top left: Paired Blackbird tracks; Lightly registered Blackbird track; Blackbird tracks in deep mud; Blackbird tracks in wet sand.

SONG THRUSH *(TURDUS PHILOMELOS)*

Track: 36mm. Classic bird track. Noticeable toe pads at the end of the Hallux and Toe 3 (albeit not quite as obvious as in Blackbird). The overall track is curved, with Toe 3 itself curving towards the centre of the trail. Toes 2 and 4 are also curved ('drooping'). The Metatarsal area rarely registers. Song Thrushes tend to skip, run and hop, and the resulting track pattern can help in identification.

Similar Species: Very similar to Blackbird tracks although about 10 per cent smaller, with a proportionately (slightly) shorter Hallux. Starling tracks are also very similar but they have more robust toes, and Toes 2 and 4 tend to be held closer to Toe 3 than in the Song Thrush, but this is not reliable.

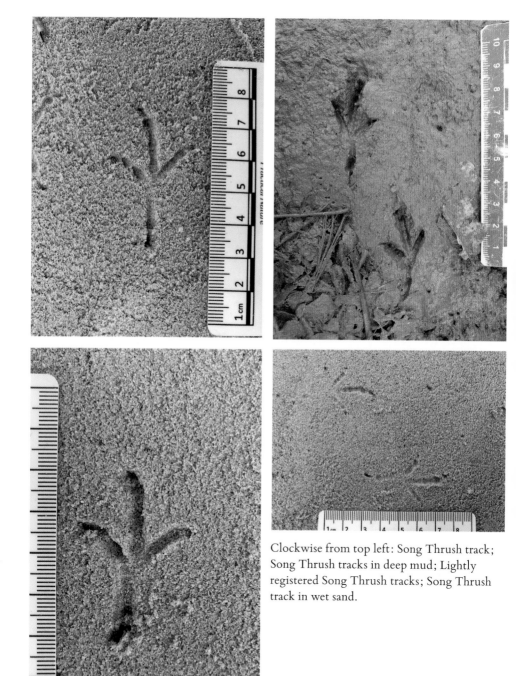

Clockwise from top left: Song Thrush track; Song Thrush tracks in deep mud; Lightly registered Song Thrush tracks; Song Thrush track in wet sand.

STARLING (*STURNUS VULGARIS*)

Track: 39mm. Classic bird track with relatively robust toes that can show noticeable pads (including at the end of the toes). The Metatarsal area rarely registers. Starlings walk, and this track pattern can help in identification.
Similar Species: Very similar to Blackbird, although Blackbird tracks are more elegant with a proportionately longer Hallux and more obvious toe pads on Toe 3 and the Hallux. See Song Thrush.

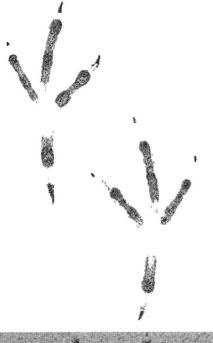

Clockwise from below: Starling tracks in sand; Lightly registered Starling tracks in clay; Multiple Starling tracks.

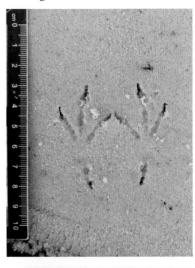

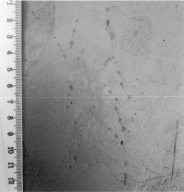

ROBIN (*ERITHACUS RUBECULA*)

Track: 26mm. Small, classic bird track with very slender toes, with bulbous ends on the Hallux and (especially) Toe 3 – like a small, thin-toed Blackbird track. Robin tracks are distinctive for the very flexible tip of Toe 3, which is frequently bent (in quite an extreme way) towards the centre of the trail. Both the toe tip and the nail bend inwards. The overall track is curved, and the Metatarsal area rarely registers. Robins hop, and the resulting track pattern can help in identification.
Similar Species: Compare with the larger Thrushes, and also the similar-sized Dunnock.

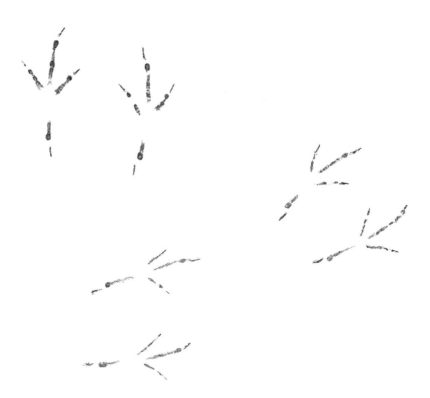

Clockwise from above: Paired Robin tracks;
Lightly registered Robin
tracks; Robin tracks in dust; Robin
tracks (x2 images);
Close-up of a Robin's feet.

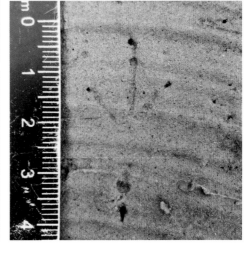

GREAT TIT (*PARUS MAJOR*)

Track: 23mm. A very narrow track with Toes 2 and 4 hugging close to Toe 3. The Hallux and Toe 2 form a straight line on the inside of the track, which is characteristic of Tits (and their New World Chickadee relatives). The Metatarsal area tends to register weakly or may be absent. The nails register reliably. Our largest Tit, and therefore the largest of the Tit tracks. **Similar Species:** Finches have curved tracks (as the Hallux and Toe 3 point in towards the centre of the trail). Compare with the larger but similar Nuthatch. Other species splay their toes more.
Notes: Based on a relatively small sample of (albeit) detailed tracks.

Below left: Great Tit tracks in clay.

Below right: Paired Great Tit tracks – Great Tits land feet together and hop. (MS)

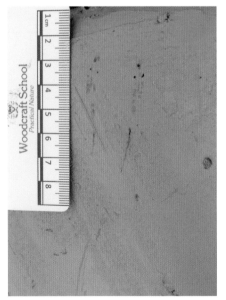

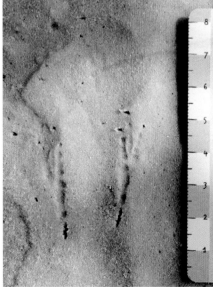

BLUE TIT (*CYANISTES CAERULEUS*)

Track: 18mm. A tiny, narrow track with Toes 2 and 4 hugging close to Toe 3. The Hallux and Toe 2 form a straight line on the inside of the track, which is characteristic of Tits although other small Passerines may also show this feature. The Metatarsal area tends to register weakly or may be absent. The nails register reliably.

Similar Species: Compare with the larger Great Tit. Finches have curved tracks (as the Hallux and Toe 3 point in towards the centre of the trail). Other species splay their toes more.

Below left: Blue Tit in the hand, showing its foot.

Below right: Blue Tit tracks.

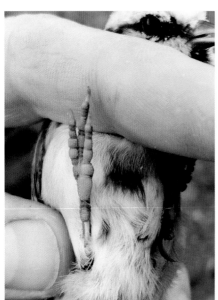

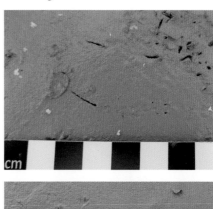

NUTHATCH *(SITTA EUROPAEA)*

Track: 28mm. A very narrow track with Toes 2 and 4 hugging close to Toe 3. All toes are slender, and the Hallux has a long nail (*c.*7mm), which is a key identification feature. The toes tend to curve slightly towards the inside. Toes 2, 3 and 4 are obviously uneven in length, and the Hallux is offset towards the inside of the track.

Similar Species: The Great Tit is just a bit smaller, the nail on the Hallux is nowhere near as long and the overall track shape is more of an acute arrowhead. Toes 2 and 4 are closer in length in the Great Tit.

Notes: Based on very few confirmed tracks, so the average length could vary, as could the typical presentation.

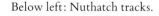
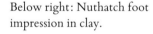

Below left: Nuthatch tracks.

Below right: Nuthatch foot impression in clay.

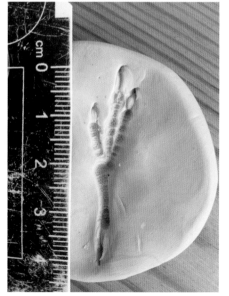

BLACKCAP (*SYLVIA ATRICAPILLA*)

Track: 22mm. A very narrow track, with Toe 3 significantly longer than those either side of it. The base of the Hallux is relatively broad and forms a long triangle shape. The Metatarsal registers weakly.

Similar Species: Other *Sylvia* Warblers may well have very similar tracks. Compare also with the Tits (where the Hallux and Toe 2 form a straight line). Finches have curved tracks.

Notes: The tracks of Warblers will be very rarely (if ever) found. We have not seen the tracks of the Blackcap in the field. This drawing was done from the tracks of a live bird that stood on a clay pad, and informed by photos of Blackcap feet and impressions cast (by Paul Wernicke) in clay.

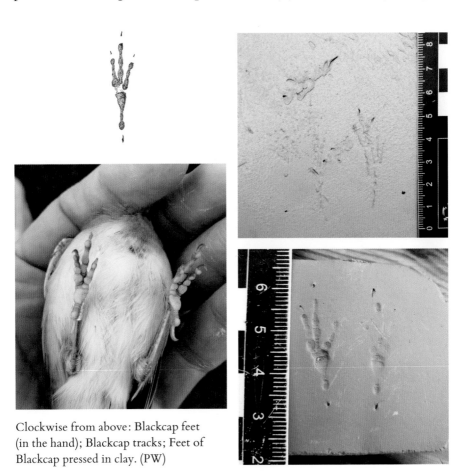

Clockwise from above: Blackcap feet (in the hand); Blackcap tracks; Feet of Blackcap pressed in clay. (PW)

CHAFFINCH (*FRINGILLA COELEBS*)

Track: 25mm. Classic Finch track with the Hallux and Toe 3 often forming a curve towards the centre of the trail. The Metatarsal area registers weakly if at all.

Similar Species: Other Finch species share the same curved track morphology, so consider size, habitat and behaviour. European Greenfinch (*Chloris chloris*) is likely to have a very similar-sized track and is probably inseparable.

Notes: Based on very few clear tracks, so the average size could vary a little.

Below left: Chaffinch feet.

Below right: Chaffinch track in the snow. (DP)

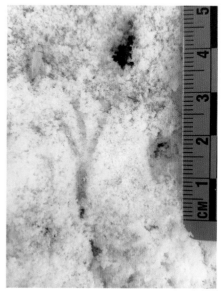

LINNET (*LINARIA CANNABINA*)

Track: 23mm. Classic Finch track with the Hallux and Toe 3 often forming a curve towards the centre of the trail. The Metatarsal area registers weakly if at all.

Similar Species: Other Finch species share the same curved track morphology, so consider size, habitat and behaviour. Probably inseparable from the Twite.

Notes: Among various habitats, Linnets often occur in sand dunes, where their hopping trails can be found quite commonly.

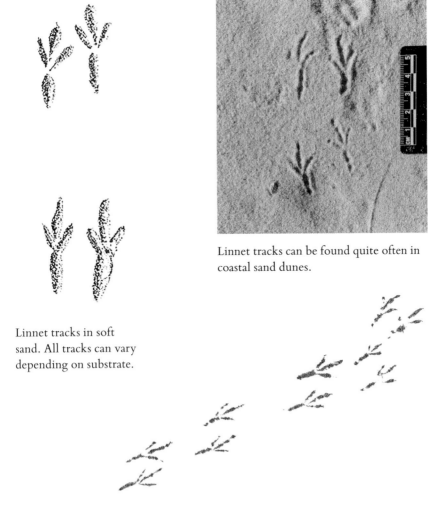

Linnet tracks can be found quite often in coastal sand dunes.

Linnet tracks in soft sand. All tracks can vary depending on substrate.

TWITE (*LINARIA FLAVIROSTRIS*)

Track: 24mm. Classic Finch track with the Hallux and Toe 3 often forming a curve towards the centre of the trail. The Metatarsal area registers weakly if at all.

Similar Species: Other Finch species share the same curved track morphology, so consider size, habitat and behaviour. Probably inseparable from the Linnet.

Notes: A rare bird of treeless moors and bare coastal heaths (and crofting lands in Scotland and Ireland). In winter many move to coastal areas (often feeding on the strand line with other Finches and Buntings), where their tracks are more likely to be encountered.

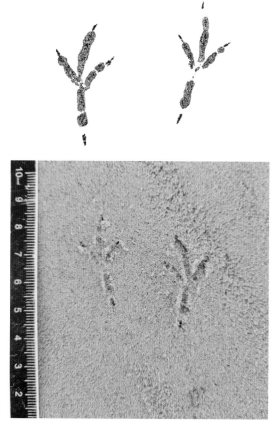

Twite tracks.

GOLDFINCH (*CARDUELIS CARDUELIS*)

Track: 20mm. Very small classic bird track with the Hallux and Toe 3 forming a curve in towards the centre of the trail (which is typical for Finches). The Metatarsal area registers weakly.

Similar Species: Other Finches show the same curved track characteristics, with species such as Mealy Redpoll (*Acanthis flammea*) and Siskin (*Spinus spinus*) probably having very similar-sized tracks.

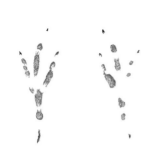

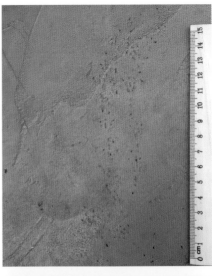

Goldfinch tracks in clay
(coming to drink beside a garden pond).

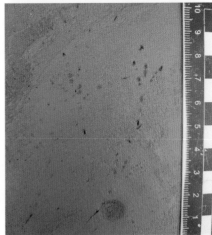

HOUSE SPARROW (*PASSER DOMESTICUS*)

Track: 25mm. Classic bird track that curves in towards the centre of the trail. Toes 2 and 4 are short (Toe 4 especially so), and the Metatarsal area tends to register weakly. House Sparrows hop, so look for pairs of tracks.
Similar Species: Finches have similar-looking tracks, although they have proportionately longer Toes 2 and 4.

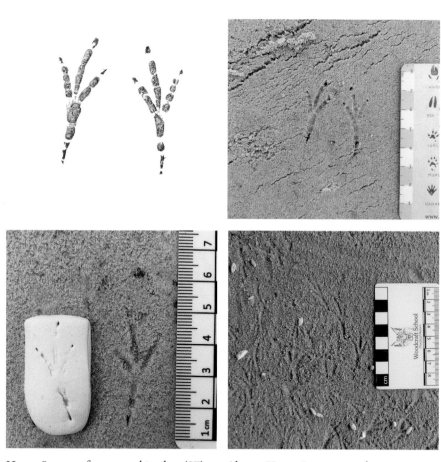

House Sparrow feet pressed in clay. (SF)   Above: House Sparrow tracks.

SNOW BUNTING (*PLECTROPHENAX NIVALIS*)

Track: 27mm. Quite a distinctive track with the Hallux and Toe 3 curving towards the centre of the trail. Toes 2 and 4 also curve – or droop. All toes have large toe pads (an adaptation for walking on sand and snow, perhaps). The Hallux and Toe 3 especially show bulbous ends in the tracks. The Hallux has a long nail. The Metatarsal registers weakly. Snow Buntings tend to skip and this is obvious in their trails.

Similar Species: Compare with Shore Lark, which sometimes mix with Snow Bunting flocks and often share the same beach habitat in winter. Shore Larks run rather than skip (Elbroch and Marks, 2001).

Notes: Found in flocks on sandy and gravelly beaches in winter and therefore do register tracks, and also signs of feeding (beak marks and scratches).

Snow Bunting foot (museum specimen) showing the bulbous toe ends.

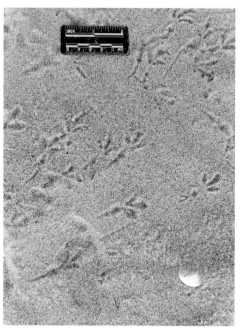

A mass of Snow Bunting tracks from a flock feeding at the strand line on a beach.

Snow Bunting track.

REED BUNTING (*EMBERIZA SCHOENICLUS*)

Track: 23mm. Slender toes, with Toe 3 curving towards the centre of the trail. Toes 2 and 4 appear to droop slightly. The Hallux is proportionately short, but with a long nail. The Metatarsal registers weakly.
Similar Species: Probably similar to Yellowhammer with which Reed Buntings flock during winter, although we have not found the tracks of Yellowhammer to compare.

Below left: Reed Bunting feet impressions in clay.

Below right: Reed Bunting tracks in sand.

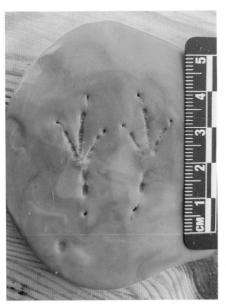

DUNNOCK (*PRUNELLA MODULARIS*)

Track: 22mm. Classic bird track with the Hallux and Toe 3 forming a curve towards the centre of the trail. The ends of the Hallux and Toe 3 have quite bulbous toe pads that seem to show in the tracks. The Metatarsal area registers weakly.

Similar Species: House Sparrow tracks are very similar but Toes 2 and 4 are obviously shorter. The Finches have tracks with an even more pronounced curve but without such bulbous toe ends.

Notes: Dunnocks hop. Description and average size measurements based on very few tracks.

Below left: Dunnock track in snow. (GC)

Below right: Paired Dunnock tracks (with larger Blackbird tracks).

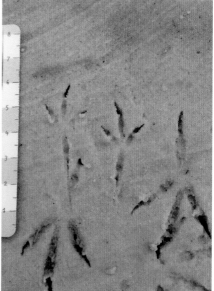

SPOTTED FLYCATCHER (*MUSCICAPA STRIATA*)

Track: 27mm. A relatively robust track with a short Hallux and long Toe 3. The tracks tend to curve in towards the centre of the trail. Spotted Flycatchers will land, feet together, to catch an insect and may hop once, but they don't like being on the ground.

Similar Species: Compare with the very similar House Sparrow and similar-sized Finches.

Notes: Confirmed tracks found once and included here for interest and information. It is doubtful if this species could be identified by its tracks alone.

Spotted Flycatcher tracks.

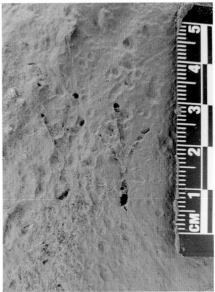

SWALLOW (*HIRUNDO RUSTICA*)

Track: 19mm. Very small. A short Hallux combined with long Toes 2, 3 and 4 held close together makes for a unique-looking track. Toe 3 is noticeably the longest, and the Metatarsal registers weakly or is absent altogether.

Similar Species: Keep the other Martins in mind (House Martin and Sand Martin) as they have feet with a similar structure.

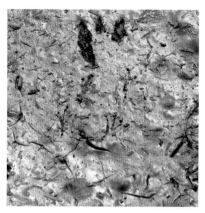

Swallow tracks can be found where they gather mud for nesting, but often leave just beak marks. (SR)

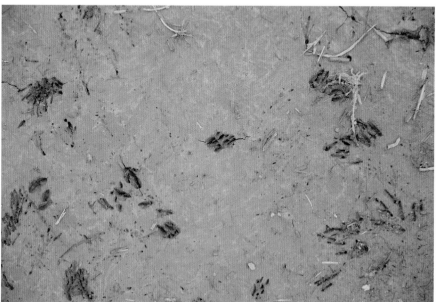

SKYLARK (*ALAUDA ARVENSIS*)

Track: 26mm. Classic bird track in which the Metatarsal registers weakly. The Hallux and Toe 3 have large (bulbous) toe pads and long nails. The Hallux especially registers as a teardrop shape because of the bulbous end to it, and the nail extends about 15mm beyond this. Toe 3 often curves in towards the centre of the trail, and thus the tracks look 'pigeon-toed'.

Similar Species: Pipits and Wagtails have a longer Hallux, and longer Toes 2 and 4. They don't have the obvious, teardrop end to the Hallux, and their tracks do not curve inwards as the Skylark's do. Skylarks walk and run, and leave a relatively straight trail in contrast to the meandering trails of Pipits and Wagtails.

Below left: Skylark track showing the long Hallux nail.

Below right: Skylark track.

SHORE LARK (*EREMOPHILA ALPESTRIS*)

Track: 25mm. Classic bird track in which the Metatarsal registers weakly. The Hallux and Toe 3 have large (bulbous) toe pads and long nails (*c*.8mm long on the Hallux and 5mm on Toe 3), which show in the tracks. Toe 3 often curves in towards the centre of the trail, and thus the tracks look 'pigeon-toed' (Elbroch and Marks, 2001).

Similar Species: See Skylark. Although the classic trail of the Shore Lark is the run, it will walk while feeding (Elbroch and Marks, 2001), and therefore could be confused with Pipits (which also walk). Pipits have a longer Hallux, no bulbous toe pads and longer Toes 2 and 4. Snow Buntings have even more bulbous ends to Toe 3 and the Hallux, and they tend to skip.

Notes: Drawn from the track photo in Elbroch and Marks (2001) and checked against museum specimens. Track size is approximate. A scarce winter visitor to sandy and gravelly beaches, where they often associate with flocks of Snow Buntings.

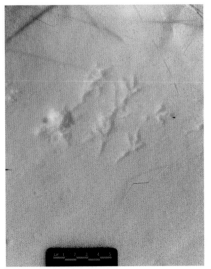 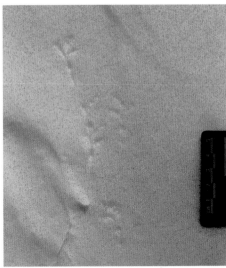

Shore Lark tracks.

MEADOW PIPIT (*ANTHUS PRATENSIS*)

Track: 30mm. Classic bird track that is notable for the very long nail on the Hallux (that is about the same length as the Hallux). This nail often leaves drag marks, making the trail quite characteristically 'Pipit'. Toe 3 and the Hallux tend to line up but can present as slightly offset (see Similar Species below). The Metatarsal area registers weakly if at all, and the tracks tend to turn in towards the centre of the trail (giving a slightly pigeon-toed appearance). Pipits tend to walk when feeding.

Similar Species: Compare with the Wagtails that have a shorter nail on the Hallux and where the Hallux is noticeably offset from Toe 3 (although be aware that Meadow Pipit tracks can sometimes look slightly offset, too). Rock Pipit has a very similar track (and may often not be separable), but look for the Rock Pipit's shorter nail on the Hallux and consider habitat.

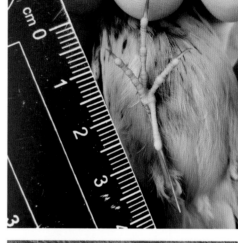

Clockwise from right: Close-up of Meadow Pipit foot. The Hallux is clearly offset, but this only sometimes shows in the tracks; Meadow Pipit track (RN); Meadow Pipit tracks in soft mud.

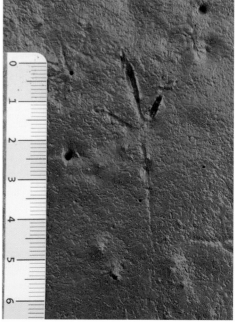

ROCK PIPIT (*ANTHUS PETROSUS*)

Track: 29mm. Classic bird track, which is notable for the long nail on the Hallux. This nail often leaves drag marks, making the trail quite characteristically 'Pipit'. Toe 3 and the Hallux tend to line up (most of the time). The Metatarsal area registers weakly if at all, and the tracks tend to turn in towards the centre of the trail (giving a slightly pigeon-toed appearance). Pipits tend to walk when feeding.

Similar Species: Meadow Pipit has a very similar track. Compare with the Wagtails that have a shorter nail on the Hallux and where the Hallux is not in line with Toe 3 (although be aware that Rock Pipit tracks can sometimes look offset, too).

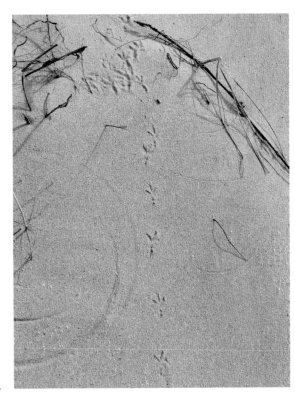

Rock Pipit trail.

PIED WAGTAIL (*MOTACILLA ALBA*)

Track: 26mm. Classic bird track in which the Hallux is obviously offset (to the inside of the track) and therefore not in line with Toe 3. This is noticeable in most (but not all) tracks. The Metatarsal area registers weakly if at all. The Hallux has a long nail that often leaves drag marks as the birds walk and run.

Similar Species: Probably inseparable from Grey Wagtail, although the Grey Wagtail has a shorter nail on the Hallux. Compare also with the Pipits.

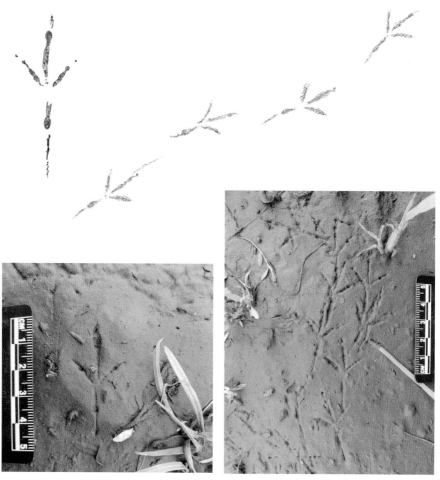

Pied Wagtail tracks. Note the tendency for the Hallux to be offset.

GREY WAGTAIL (*MOTACILLA CINEREA*)

Track: 23mm. Classic bird track in which the Hallux is obviously offset (to the inside of the track) and therefore not in line with Toe 3. This appears to be noticeable in most tracks. The Metatarsal area registers weakly if at all. The Hallux has a long nail that often leaves drag marks as the birds walk.
Similar Species: Probably inseparable from Pied Wagtail, although the Pied Wagtail has a longer nail on the Hallux. Compare also with the Pipits.
Notes: Drawing and measurements based on tracks from just one bird.

Grey Wagtail track.

WREN (*TROGLODYTES TROGLODYTES*)

Track: 24mm. Surprisingly large track for such a small bird. The Hallux is long, and appears even longer due to the long nail. Toes 2 and 4 are held quite close to Toe 3, and the overall track tends to be curved (the Hallux and Toe 3 pointing inwards toward the centre of the trail). The Metatarsal area registers weakly. Wrens tend to hop.

Similar Species: Tracks of other similar-sized species have a shorter Hallux in proportion to the overall track length.

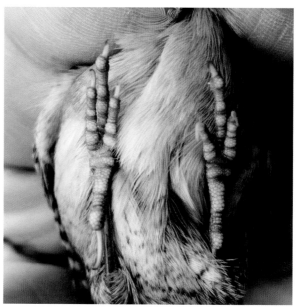

Wren feet.

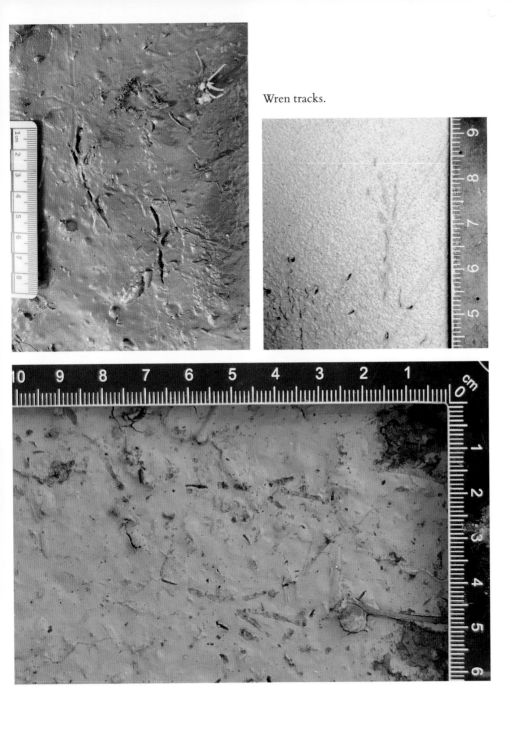

Wren tracks.

SYNDACTYL BIRDS

Track type: Syndactyl.
Track size: Small (18mm).
Key features: Toes 3 and 4 are fused along their basal half.

SPECIES

Common Kingfisher *Alcedo atthis*

These are very similar to classic bird tracks except that Toes 3 and 4 are fused for much of their length. We describe only one species in this group – the Common Kingfisher – which is unique among our resident birds in its foot structure.

SYNDACTYL TRACK DESCRIPTION

COMMON KINGFISHER (*ALCEDO ATTHIS*)

Track: 18mm. Unique among our resident birds, Kingfishers have Syndactyl feet. Three toes point forwards and a relatively robust Hallux points backwards. Toe 2 is much reduced and Toes 3 and 4 are fused from their base to (about) halfway up, after which they are separate toes. Toe 3 is the longest. The foot is quite wide across the Metatarsal area, but it is likely that the Metatarsal registers weakly if at all (see Notes).
Similar Species: European Bee-eater (*Merops apiaster*) has a similar Syndactyl foot structure, albeit seemingly more robust and larger (*c*.30mm long) (Abenza García, 2018). Compare also with Blue Tit and Great Tit, and consider location.

Notes: Drawn from a foot impression in clay (with thanks to Paul Wernicke) and checked against a live bird caught under license for ringing. We've never seen the tracks of the Kingfisher, although it is not implausible that tracks would be left by birds sitting on riversides. One to search for! The tracks of Belted Kingfisher (*Ceryle alcyon*) from North America register the Metatarsal weakly if at all (Elbroch and Marks, 2001).

The Kingfisher's unique Syndactyl feet.

Kingfisher foot impressions in clay. (PW)

PIGEONS AND DOVES

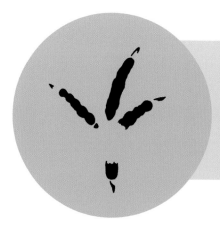

Track type: Classic.
Track size: Large (38–56mm).
Key features: Obvious curve from Hallux to Toe 3 towards the centre of the trail. Metatarsal area often absent, leaving a large negative space.

SPECIES

Wood Pigeon *Columba palumbus*
Stock Dove *Columba oenas*
Turtle Dove *Streptopelia turtur*

Rock Dove/Feral Pigeon *Columba livia*
Collared Dove *Streptopelia decaocto*

The tracks of Pigeons and Doves are found commonly and are very identifiable as 'one of the pigeons', if not to species level. As a group, the Pigeons (across the world, not just in Britain) have track characteristics that are unique and obvious once you get your eye in. The most obvious feature is that they are 'pigeon-toed' – an expression that is used to describe humans that walk with their toes pointing inwards, and which relates (in Pigeons) to the very distinct curve from the Hallux (Toe 1) right through to Toe 3; a curve that arcs towards the centre of the trail. The outer toe (Toe 4) is spread out at a wide angle and the Metatarsal area is most often absent, leaving a large negative space. The toes, proportional to the size of the track, usually show as quite strong and robust. These features hold true across the group, from the largest (Wood Pigeon) to the smallest (Turtle Dove). When the arcing tracks of Pigeons combine in a trail, they form a distinctive 'snaking' pattern that is also an important aid to identification.

Members of the Pigeon family have very distinct tracks and trails.

PIGEONS AND DOVES TRACK DESCRIPTIONS

WOOD PIGEON *(COLUMBA PALUMBUS)*

Track: 56mm. The classic Pigeon track, and the largest of these to be found in the British Isles. Relatively robust toes with the pad segments often showing in the track. Classically curved along the length of the track (from the Hallux to the tip of Toe 3). Toe 2 is relatively close to Toe 3, and the thinner, longer Toe 4 sticks out to the side and often appears to 'droop' (curve downwards). The Metatarsal area and the base of the Hallux rarely register (except in deep substrates), but the terminal pad of the Hallux registers quite reliably, as do the nails.

Similar Species: Only confusable with the larger doves (Rock Dove/Feral Pigeon and Stock Dove), which, with practice, do appear slightly smaller.

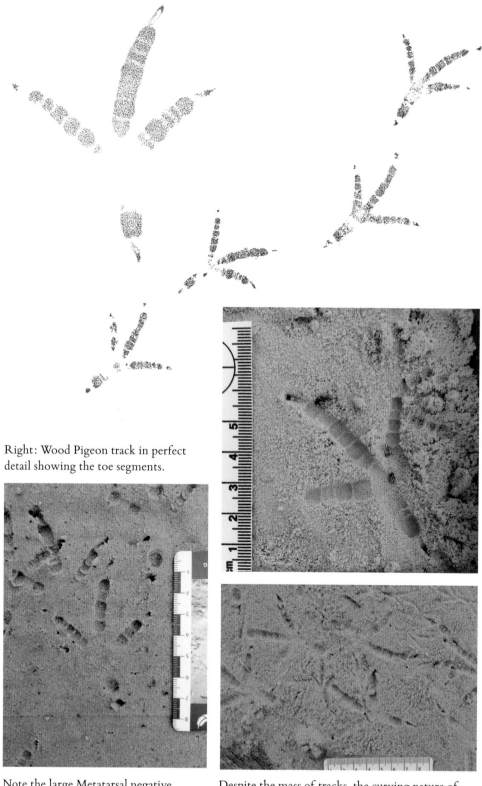

Right: Wood Pigeon track in perfect detail showing the toe segments.

Note the large Metatarsal negative space on this Wood Pigeon track.

Despite the mass of tracks, the curving nature of both the trail and the individual tracks can be seen.

ROCK DOVE/FERAL PIGEON *(COLUMBA LIVIA)*

Track: 53mm. Essentially the same as Wood Pigeon, albeit a little smaller.
Similar Species: Probably not separable from the Wood Pigeon with any confidence in the field, and may overlap with the slightly smaller Stock Dove.

Rock Dove tracks and trail.

STOCK DOVE (*COLUMBA OENAS*)

Track: 49mm. Essentially a small version of a Wood Pigeon track.
Similar Species: Tracks average 10 per cent smaller than Wood Pigeon, which is noticeable when fully familiar with the larger species.
Notes: Track size is based on just a small handful of tracks, so the species average could vary subtly.

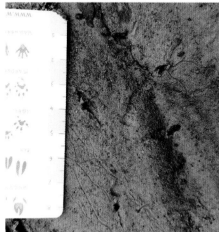

Right top: Faintly registered Stock Dove track.

Right bottom: Stock Dove track.

COLLARED DOVE *(STREPTOPELIA DECAOCTO)*

Track: 38mm. The smallest Dove track, still showing all of the classic track features of this group.
Similar Species: The size of Collared Dove tracks puts them in the range of other Passerine species that can appear superficially similar. In particular, keep in mind the Blackbird and Starling, and use the trail to help with an identification.
See also Turtle Dove.

Collared Dove tracks.

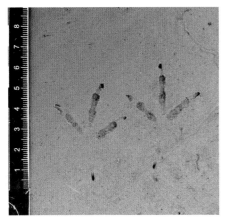

Collared Dove tracks.

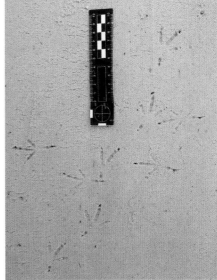

Collared Dove trail
with a Blackbird crossing it.

TURTLE DOVE (*STREPTOPELIA TURTUR*)

Track: 40mm. The tracks of Turtle Dove appear identical to those of the Collared Dove, and it is unclear whether they can be separated reliably in the field.

Similar Species: See Collared Dove.

Notes: Drawn from track photos in Brown et al. (2013) and a foot impression in Bergmann and Klaus (2016). The Turtle Dove is a smaller bird than the Collared Dove – 20 per cent smaller – and with measuring a greater number of confirmed tracks this size difference may become apparent. Only one track was measured here (although the size was consistent with museum specimen foot measurements). The Turtle Dove is an increasingly rare summer visitor, so small Dove tracks should be assumed to belong to the Collared Dove until proven otherwise.

CROWS

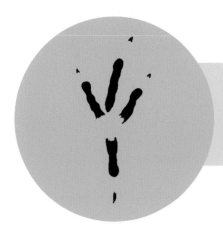

Track type: Classic.
Track size: Large to Very Large (48–82mm).
Key features: Toe 2 hugging Toe 3.

SPECIES

Raven *Corvus corax*
Carrion Crow *Corvus corone*
Red-billed Chough *Pyrrhocorax pyrrhocorax*
Magpie *Pica pica*

Hooded Crow *Corvus cornix*
Rook *Corvus frugilegus*
Jackdaw *Coloeus monedula*
Jay *Garrulus glandarius*

All the British Crows (or Corvids) leave classic bird tracks, with three toes pointing forwards (Toes 2, 3 and 4) and one back (the Hallux, or Toe 1). The obvious pads of their segmented toes show in the tracks of all species (in favourable substrates), and the Metatarsal area tends to register weakly or not at all.

Aside from the Jay, all the other Corvids commonly show Toes 2 and 3 in close proximity to each other (Toe 3 bent or angled slightly towards the inside, and Toe 2 inclined towards it), a feature that is often referred to by trackers as the 'hugging inner toe'. This typical Corvid track configuration of hugging toes (Toes 2 and 3) with Toe 4 projecting out to the side, makes it very unlikely for tracks of the Corvid species to be confused with anything other than each other, with the possible exception of the tracks of Raven (see below).

Within this group, Rook, Carrion and Hooded Crows are most easily confused with each other as they are of a similar size. Carrion Crow tracks are the most common robust Corvid tracks encountered. They often spend time on the ground, and in soft substrate frequently show a drag mark from the large nail on the Hallux. Familiarity with Carrion Crow tracks will allow the tracker to use their tracks as a baseline from which to notice if a Corvid track is 'smaller or larger than normal'.

Rooks are slight in comparison, and shorter, which makes their tracks appear a little 'stunted' when compared with Carrion Crows. The Hooded Crow is very similar to the Carrion Crow and it is probably impossible to reliably split these species, although Hooded Crows are slightly larger and more robust on average and this may appear in the track.

Confusion exists amongst the smaller Corvids – namely Jackdaw, Magpie, and Red-billed Chough, which are similar in size. The latter is very specific in its habitat requirements, being most likely encountered in rocky coastal or mountain areas with short grass. It can therefore be discounted as a possibility in most areas of the country.

The Red-billed Chough is the largest of these smaller Corvids, perhaps reaching close to Rook size. Their bulbous toe pads on the ends of the Hallux and Toe 3 register well in good substrate and may be diagnostic.

Jackdaw and Magpie tracks are very similar in size and it may not always be possible to separate these species. Toe 2, when a difference can be noted, is shorter on a Magpie. A useful technique is to imagine a line running from the top of Toe 4 to the top of Toe 2. On a Jackdaw this line would be perpendicular to the Hallux. On a Magpie it is canted down towards the centre of the trail. Because of this, the Hallux of the Magpie appears out of line with Toe 3.

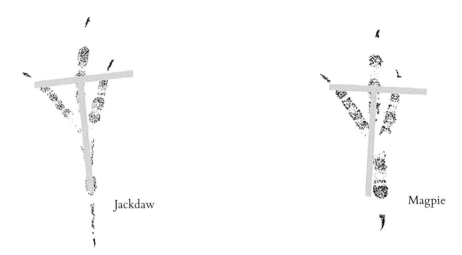

Jackdaw

Magpie

Our largest Corvid, the Raven, is more likely to be confused with a Bird of Prey such as a Red Kite or Common Buzzard rather than another Corvid species due to its large size. Look for the Raven's longer Hallux and less bulbous pad on the Hallux. On Birds of Prey this pad is very noticeable, but with the Raven, the Hallux resembles an ice cream cone (or wedge) tapering down to the nail.

Jay tracks are the exception to the classic Corvid track pattern, as they present both the inner and the outer toes (Toes 2 and 4) very close to the leading toe (Toe 3). This is also the case with several smaller tree-dwelling species including the Tits and Nuthatch. However, this feature coupled with the Jay's large size and paired hopping gait in fact makes the Jay perhaps the most easily recognisable and least confusable of all the Corvid species.

CROWS TRACK DESCRIPTIONS

RAVEN (*CORVUS CORAX*)

Track: 82mm. Typical Corvid track, the large size of which is striking and diagnostic.

Similar Species: Even though the structure is essentially the same, Raven tracks are reliably separated from other Corvids on size alone, being 30 per cent larger than the next largest species. Common Buzzard tracks are superficially similar but the Hallux is relatively shorter in the Buzzard, and the Metatarsal area of the track is much broader.

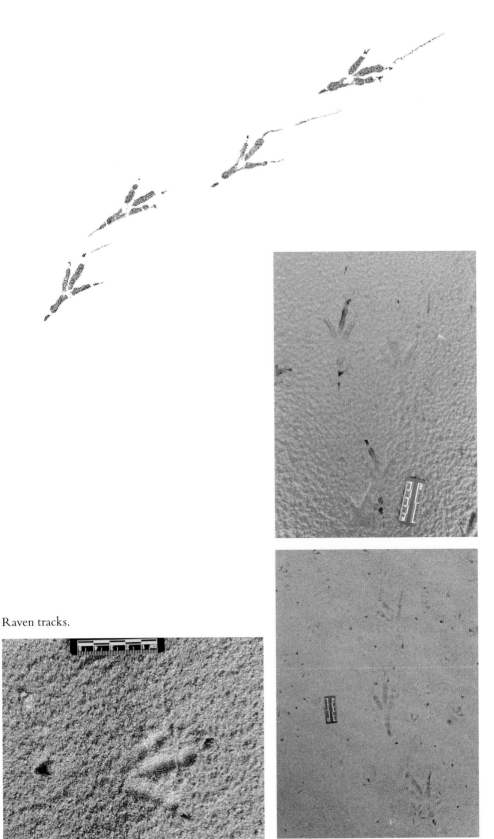

Raven tracks.

HOODED CROW (*CORVUS CORNIX*)

Track: 65mm. Large, typical Corvid. The long nail on the Hallux often leaves drag marks in softer substrates.

Similar Species: Hooded Crow tracks are near identical to Carrion Crow tracks (see Notes below), although they appear, on average, slightly larger. See Carrion Crow for other similar species.

Notes: The Hooded Crow was only recently split taxonomically from the Carrion Crow (Parkin et al., 2003), and it is not surprising that these two species have near identical tracks. Hooded Crows (in the British Isles) are confined to north and west Scotland (including the western and northern isles) and Ireland, so large Corvid tracks in these areas are likely to be this species. Within Europe, Hooded Crow populations become gradually larger in size to the west and north.

Hooded Crow trail – note the Hallux nail drag.

The right track of a Hooded Crow.

CARRION CROW (*CORVUS CORONE*)

Track: 62mm. Large, typical Corvid track. The long nail on the Hallux often leaves drag marks in softer substrates such as sand and mud (although note that other Corvids will also drag the nail on their Hallux).
Similar Species: Most Corvids make similar tracks, but Carrion Crow tracks are large and robust and their size alone should separate them from the smaller tracks of Rooks (see Rook). Raven tracks are 30 per cent longer.

The right track of a Carrion Crow.

A Carrion Crow has walked across rabbit tracks.

ROOK *(CORVUS FRUGILEGUS)*

Track: 58mm. Medium-size, typical Corvid track.
Similar Species: In terms of size, Rook tracks sit between the 'small' Corvids (Jackdaw and Magpie) and the Carrion Crow. The tracks are robust, and therefore give the sense that this is a larger Corvid, so separation from the Carrion Crow should be done with care. Structurally it appears that Toe 3 is relatively shorter than in the Carrion Crow.

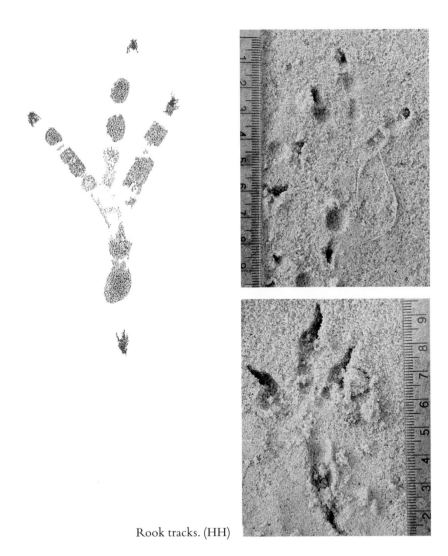

Rook tracks. (HH)

141

RED-BILLED CHOUGH (*PYRRHOCORAX PYRRHOCORAX*)

Track: 54mm. Medium-size, typical Corvid track with Toes 2 and 3 hugging (albeit possibly less prominently than other Corvids). Toe pads at the ends of Toes 1 and 3 appear to be more bulbous than in other Corvids, which may be diagnostic.

Similar Species: Very similar to Jackdaw and Magpie tracks. On average slightly larger than these 'small' Corvids (and similar in size to Rook), although there is overlap, so care should be taken in a species-level identification.

Notes: The Red-billed Chough is a rare bird of the coast along the western fringes of the British Isles (with some in the mountains of north Wales). However, it was previously more widely distributed, and with this in mind there are efforts (by Wildwood Trust and Kent Wildlife Trust) to re-establish a population in Kent, which may result in the species re-colonising the south coast. Track drawing and description based on very few tracks.

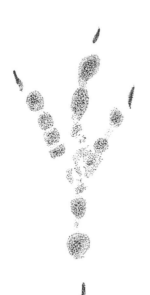
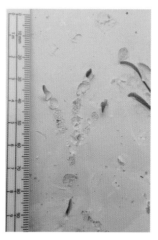

Paired Red-billed Chough tracks. (SK)

Red-billed Chough, left track. (JD & HW)

JACKDAW (*COLOEUS MONEDULA*)

Track: 49mm. Small, typical Corvid track.
Similar Species: Very similar in size and structure to the Magpie, although Toe 2 is longer in the Jackdaw than Magpie, resulting in a subtle difference in symmetry.

Right: Jackdaw track and trail. (MS)

Jackdaw left foot.

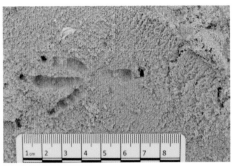

MAGPIE (*PICA PICA*)

Track: 48mm. Small, typical Corvid track.
Similar Species: Very similar in size and structure to the Jackdaw, and the tracks of these two species may often be inseparable in the field. However, there is a difference between them in the lengths of Toe 2, with this being shorter in the Magpie, resulting in a subtly different look and symmetry.

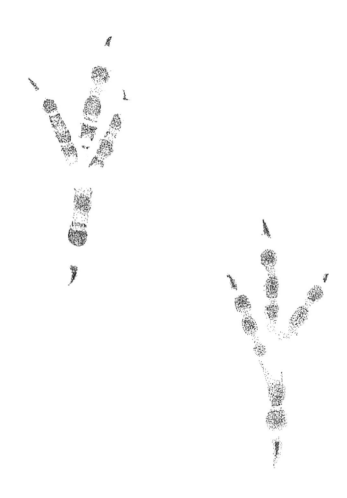

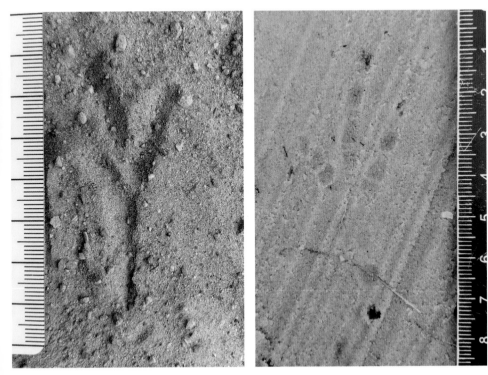

Magpie tracks.

JAY (*GARRULUS GLANDARIUS*)

Track: 46mm. Jay tracks look like a miniature trident with Toes 2, 3 and 4 held close together, facing forwards. On harder substrates the Metatarsal area registers weakly, but the well-developed toe pad at the end of the Hallux shows reliably, as do the other toes.

Similar Species: A number of small Passerines have a similar foot structure (e.g., the Tits and Nuthatch), but nothing else looking like this with tracks this size occurs in the British Isles.

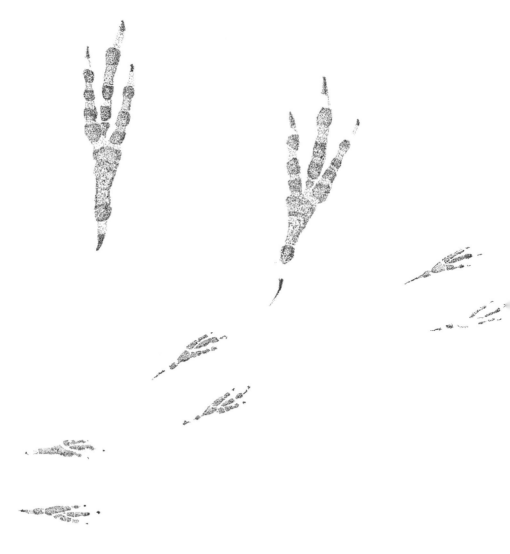

Jay tracks.

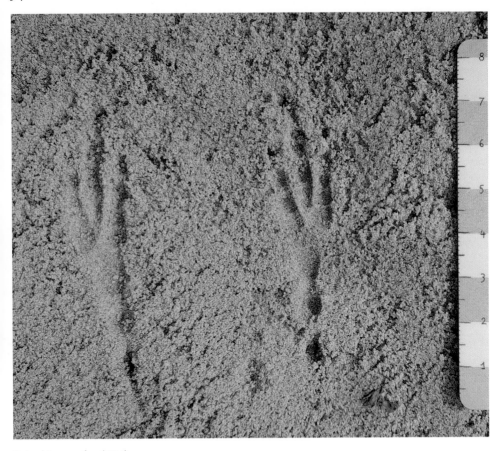

Paired Jay tracks. (KM)

BIRDS OF PREY

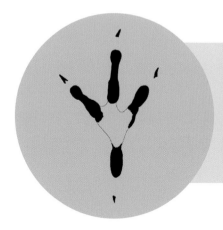

Track type: Classic.
Track size: Large to Very Large (48–130mm).
Key features:Short Hallux with large toe pad. Obvious claws.
Hallux offset from the line of Toe 3.

SPECIES

White-tailed Eagle *Haliaeetus albicilla*
Red Kite *Milvus milvus*
Common Buzzard *Buteo buteo*
Sparrowhawk *Accipiter nisus*
Peregrine *Falco peregrinus*
Merlin *Falco columbarius*

Golden Eagle *Aquila chrysaetos*
Marsh Harrier *Circus aeruginosus*
Goshawk *Accipiter gentilis*
Gyrfalcon *Falco rusticolus*
Kestrel *Falco tinnunculus*

Birds of Prey all exhibit a classic bird track arrangement with the Hallux showing in the track. The Hallux is surprisingly short in this group but is equipped with a noticeably large claw that will show in good substrates. This works in conjunction with Toe 4, which has a large claw and a robust toe pad, to administer the *coup de grâce* on its prey. Birds of Prey seldom leave good tracks on the ground and we have relied heavily on captive birds to make our comparisons. Our experience suggests the most common Bird of Prey tracks found are likely to be from Common Buzzards and (where they occur) White-tailed Eagles. However, depending on your region and the presence or absence of snow, this may vary. Keep in mind that there is considerable sexual dimorphism by size in Birds of Prey, with the females often considerably larger than males, which is reflected in their tracks.

Eagles: Usually easy to tell from their sheer size, and we have two species in the British Isles. These birds hunt but also scavenge and therefore finding their tracks in these circumstances becomes increasingly likely with the reintroduction of the White-tailed Eagle, and the increasing range of Golden Eagles. They both have partial webbing between Toes 3 and 4 and very bulbous toe pads, especially on the ends of the Hallux and Toe 2. White-tailed Eagles are making a gradual comeback in the British Isles thanks to reintroduction projects. They often land on mud and sand at the coast and beside wetlands, where they will leave tracks. Female White-tailed Eagles are 25 per cent heavier and 15 per cent longer than males, in Golden Eagles these figures are 20 per cent heavier and 10 per cent longer (Snow and Perrins, 1998). This sexual dimorphism will be reflected in the size of the tracks, and given this size range of both species, there could be a crossover in track size. Track size and drawing of the Golden Eagle is based on a single track from a captive bird.

Red Kite and Marsh Harrier: These two species are similar in size and shape to Common Buzzards but they tend to show Toe 4 held closer to 90° from Toe 3, giving the track an asymmetrical appearance. They are similar to Owls in this regard. The Hallux also curves out a little towards the outside of the body, and with Toe 3 curving in, this gives a slight 'S-shape' to the line between these two toes. Our sizes and drawings are based on single tracks of captive birds, with detail informed by the foot from a dead bird in the case of the Red Kite. Do keep in mind that both female Red Kites and Marsh Harriers are 10–15 per cent larger than males, and there is significant variation in the size of individuals (Snow and Perrins, 1998) that will be reflected in the size of their tracks. Red Kites commonly feed on the ground and will leave tracks in suitable substrate, and similarly Marsh Harriers will land on muddy substrates in wetlands, although we have not found the tracks of either species in the field yet.

Common Buzzard: Similar to Goshawk in general size and appearance, but Toes 2 and 4 are much more symmetrical in relation to the central Toe 3, as Toe 2 does not appear to hug it in quite the same way as with the Hawks. The Metatarsal area registers weakly. Webbing is not present between any of the toes (unlike the Hawks) and there are no additional fleshy appendages on the toes. The Hallux is quite short compared to a Raven, which could be a confusion species. Check also Red Kites for crossover features in identification. Female Buzzards are 5–10 per cent larger than males (Snow and Perrins, 1998), and with considerable size variation between individuals this will be reflected in the size of the tracks. Buzzards commonly feed on the ground (hunting for worms and beetles, approaching carrion or beside caught prey) and therefore will often leave tracks in suitable substrate.

Hawks: There are two species of Hawk found in our region – the common and widespread Sparrowhawk and the more localised Goshawk. Compared with Falcons, their Hallux is longer and registers more strongly. The inner Toe 2 is also held close to Toe 3, and there is some proximal webbing present between Toes 3 and 4 on both species. We have also noticed a fleshy protrusion on Toe 3 on these Hawks which may be diagnostic. The distal pad on the Hallux is very robust. Both female Goshawks and Sparrowhawks are 20 per cent larger than the males (Snow and Perrins, 1998), which will be reflected in the size of the tracks. Track sizes and drawings based on single tracks of captive female birds, with detail informed from the feet of dead birds.

Falcons: Falcons can be characterised in general terms by their relatively long, slender toes, with the Hallux registering weakly and Toe 3 describing a distinct curve towards the centre of the trail. Toe 2 is held close to Toe 3 in a similar way to the Crows (Corvids). The Metatarsal area in all four species studied registered strongly. As with the other Birds of Prey, there is sexual dimorphism related to size in the Falcons, and this may be reflected in the size of the tracks. So, female Gyrfalcons are 10 per cent larger than males, and much heavier; female Peregrines are 15 per cent larger than males; female Merlins are 10 per cent larger; while the size difference in Kestrels will probably not be noticeable (Snow and Perrins, 1998). Gyrfalcon is a bird of the northern tundra and a vagrant to the British Isles, but is included here as captive birds are sometimes found free-flying. Track sizes and drawings have been based on single tracks of captive birds (the sexes of which are mentioned in the Species descriptions).

BIRDS OF PREY TRACK DESCRIPTIONS

WHITE-TAILED EAGLE (*HALIAEETUS ALBICILLA*)

Track: 130mm (female). A huge, robust raptor track. The toe pads are bulbous and rough (which should be obvious in good substrates). The pads on the Hallux and Toe 2 are especially large. Toe 2 is angled closer to Toe 3 than the less robust Toe 4. The Metatarsal area registers weakly if at all. Talons are large and will register strongly in the track.
Similar Species: Other raptors (except Golden Eagle) have smaller tracks. Compare with the slender-toed Herons and Egrets, with which it often shares habitat.

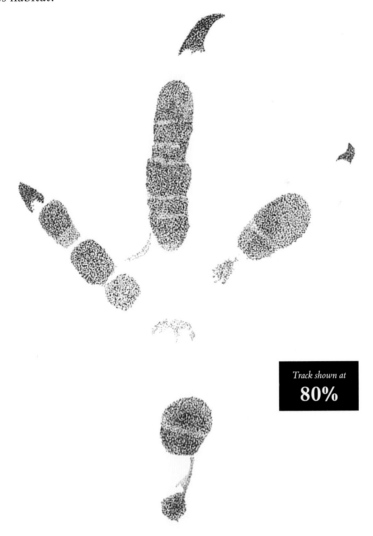

Track shown at
80%

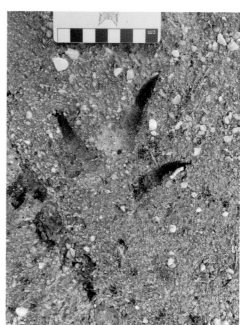

Above: White-tailed Eagle track. (AP)

Right: White-tailed Eagle tracks.

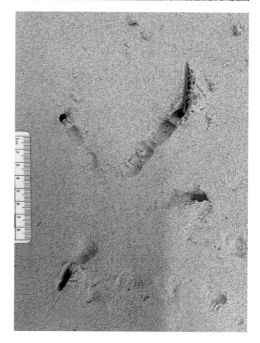

GOLDEN EAGLE (*AQUILA CHRYSAETOS*)

Track: 130mm (male). A huge, robust raptor track. The toe pads are bulbous and rough (which should be obvious in good substrates). The pads on the Hallux and Toe 2 are especially large. Toe 2 is angled closer to Toe 3 than the less robust Toe 4. The Metatarsal area registers weakly if at all. Talons are large and will register strongly in the track.
Similar Species: Other raptors (except White-tailed Eagle) have smaller tracks.

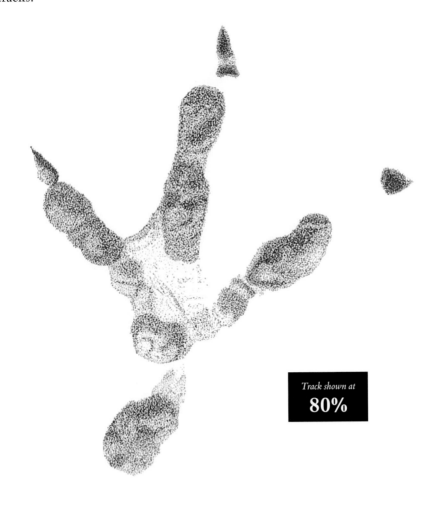

Track shown at
80%

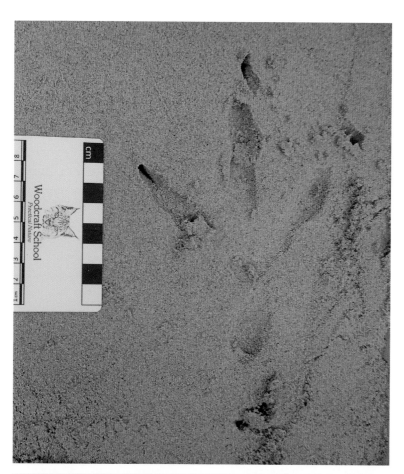

Golden Eagle tracks.

RED KITE (*MILVUS MILVUS*)

Track: 74mm. A medium-sized raptor track. The toes are robust with obvious toe pads (appearing rough in texture in good substrate), with the pads on the Hallux and Toe 2 being the most bulbous. The Hallux is offset slightly from Toe 3 towards the inside of the trail. Toe 2 is held quite close to (almost 'hugging') Toe 3, while Toe 4 is held out to the side. The Metatarsal area registers weakly if at all. Talons are large and often register strongly in the track.

Similar Species: Most similar to Common Buzzard, which averages slightly smaller, but with more robust toes and bulbous toe pads. Similar to Raven tracks with Toe 2 hugging Toe 3, but Raven tracks have less bulbous toes and the Hallux is in line with Toe 3.

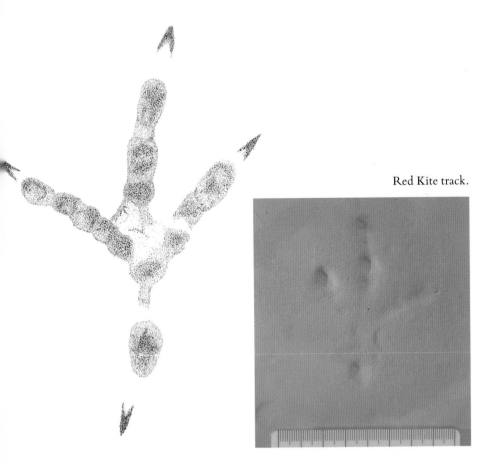

Red Kite track.

155

MARSH HARRIER *(CIRCUS AERUGINOSUS)*

Track: 82mm. A large raptor track with robust toes and obvious toe pads (appearing rough in texture in good substrate). The pads on the Hallux and Toe 2 are the most bulbous, and Toe 2 is held quite close to (almost 'hugging') Toe 3. In contrast, Toe 4 sticks out to the side at a right angle (90°) from Toe 3, which may give the tracks an 'Owl-like' appearance. However, the positioning of Toe 4 appears to be variable. The Metatarsal area registers weakly if at all. Talons are large and register strongly in the track.

Similar Species: Structurally most similar to the Red Kite, which averages smaller, and with Toe 4 held at a shallower angle than in the Marsh Harrier. Consider habitat if presented with tracks to identify.

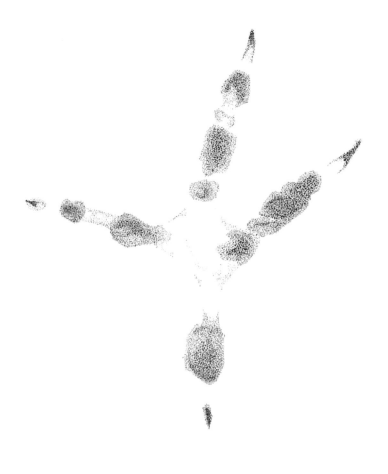

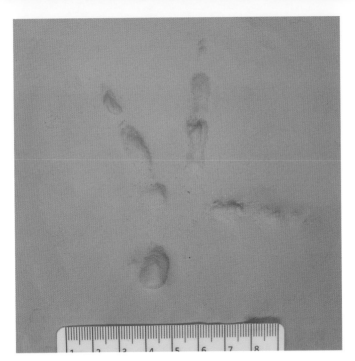

Marsh Harrier track and cast.

COMMON BUZZARD (*BUTEO BUTEO*)

Track: 66–73mm. A medium-sized raptor track with robust toes. The toe pads are large, bulbous and obvious (appearing rough in texture in good substrate), with the Hallux pad particularly so. The Hallux is offset slightly from Toe 3 towards the inside of the trail. Toe 2 is held quite close to (almost 'hugging') Toe 3, while Toe 4 is held out to the side although its position is variable. The Metatarsal area registers weakly if at all. Talons are large and often register strongly in the track.

Similar Species: Most similar to the Red Kite, which averages slightly larger, but with less robust toes and toe pads, and with Toe 4 held closer to 90° from Toe 3. Similar to Raven tracks with Toe 2 hugging Toe 3, but Raven tracks are narrower, longer, with less bulbous toes, and the Hallux is in line with Toe 3.

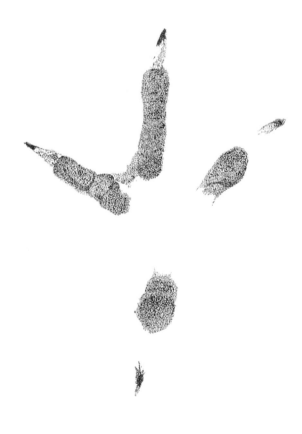

Buzzard track.

Buzzard tracks. (RA)

GOSHAWK (*ACCIPITER GENTILIS*)

Track: 104mm. A very large raptor track with big, bulbous toe pads. The Hallux toe pad is particularly large and obvious. The Hallux is offset slightly from Toe 3 towards the inside of the trail. Toe 2 is held quite close to Toe 3, while Toe 4 is held out to the side at a much greater angle. The Metatarsal area registers weakly if at all. Talons are large and often register strongly in the track.

Similar Species: Size alone separates this from other similar species. Toe 4 is proportionately longer than in other raptor tracks (such as Common Buzzard and Red Kite).

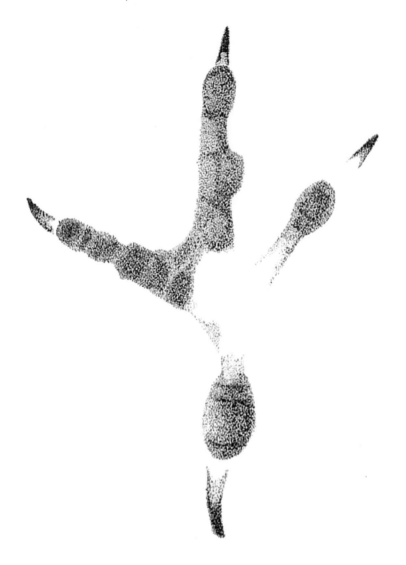

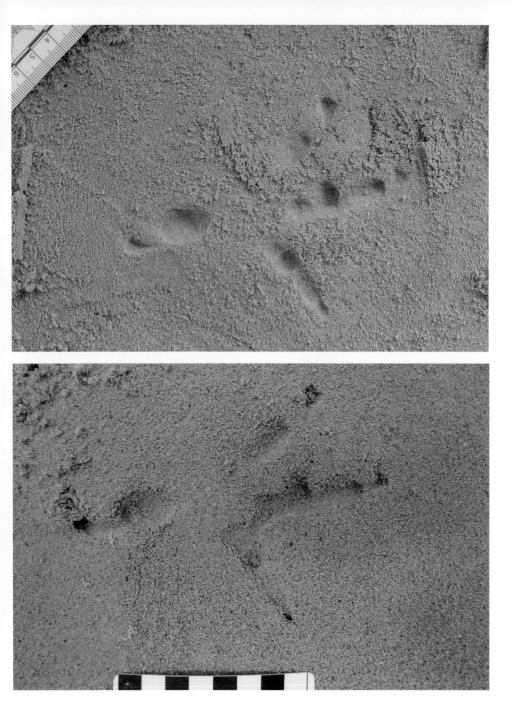

Goshawk tracks.

SPARROWHAWK (*ACCIPITER NISUS*)

Track: 65mm. A small- to medium-sized raptor track with long, slender toes and obvious toe pads. The Hallux is offset slightly from Toe 3 towards the inside of the trail. Toe 2 is held quite close to (almost 'hugging') Toe 3, while Toe 4 is held out to the side at a much greater angle. The Metatarsal area registers weakly if at all. Talons are long and needle-like.

Similar Species: Tracks (of females at least) approach those of the Common Buzzard in terms of size. Compare also with the Falcon (*Falco*) species.

Sparrowhawk tracks have an extra 'lump' on the leading Toe 3 (as have those of the Goshawk).

Sparrowhawk track cast.

GYRFALCON (*FALCO RUSTICOLUS*)

Track: 87mm (male). A large raptor track with well-defined pads along the length of relatively robust toes. The Metatarsal pad is proportionately large and appears to register. The Hallux is short, and Toe 3 relatively long and angled (perhaps with a slight curve) slightly towards the inside of the track. Talons are large and register in the track.

Similar Species: Very similar to but larger than the closely related Peregrine. Compare with other raptors of a similar size (such as Red Kite and Common Buzzard), the tracks of which show a longer Hallux and Toe 2, are more robust and don't seem to show such a prominent Metatarsal pad.

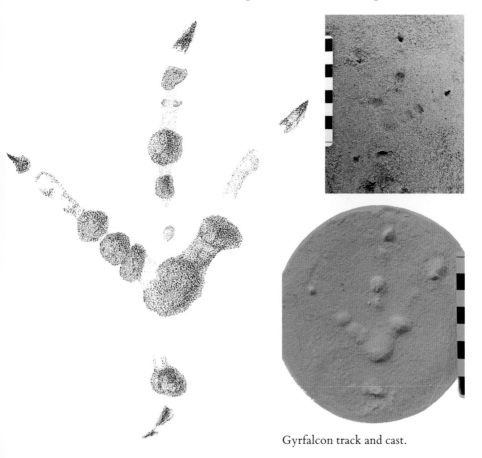

Gyrfalcon track and cast.

PEREGRINE FALCON (*FALCO PEREGRINUS*)

Track: 83mm (male). A large raptor track with well-defined pads along the length of the long toes. The Metatarsal pad is proportionately large and appears to register. The Hallux is short, and Toe 3 relatively long and angled (perhaps with a slight curve) towards the inside of the track (almost 'pigeon-toed'). Talons are large and register in the track.
Similar Species: Compare with other raptors of a similar size (such as Red Kite and Common Buzzard).

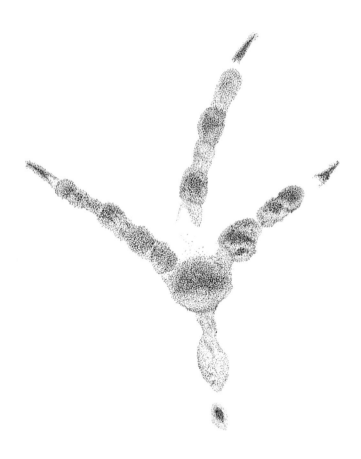

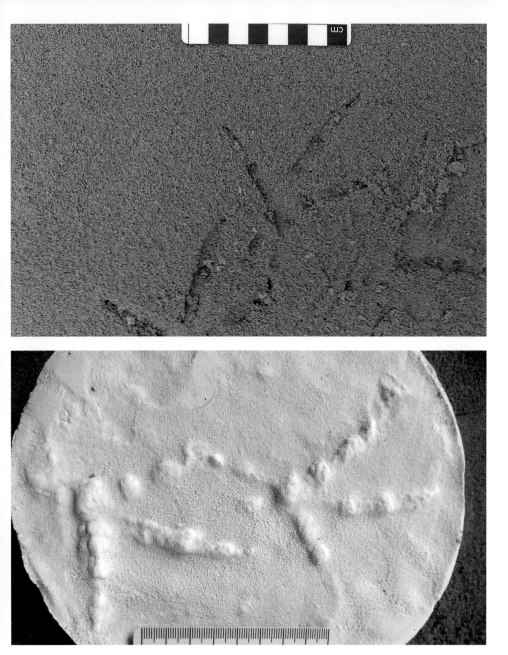

Peregrine Falcon track and cast.

KESTREL (*FALCO TINNUNCULUS*)

Track: 50mm (male). A small raptor track with obvious pads along the length of relatively robust toes. The Metatarsal pad is proportionately large and appears to register. The Hallux is short, and Toe 3 relatively long and angled (perhaps with a slight curve) towards the inside of the track (almost 'pigeon-toed'). Talons are large and register in the track.

Similar Species: Very similar in size and general shape to the Wood Pigeon, but the Wood Pigeon doesn't show the obvious toe pads, and the curves of the toes are 'smoother'. Compare with Merlin.

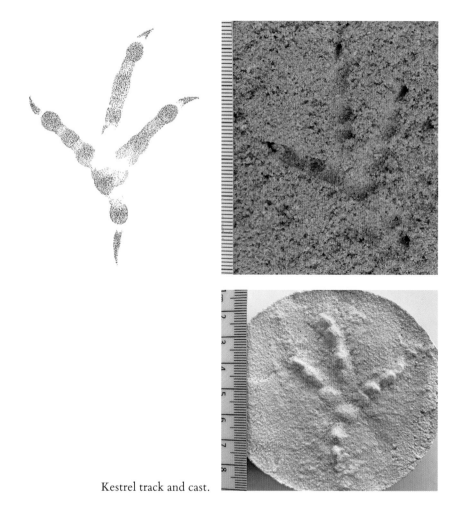

Kestrel track and cast.

MERLIN *(FALCO COLUMBARIUS)*

Track: 48mm (female). A small raptor track with relatively slender toes that show well-defined pads along their length. The Metatarsal pad is proportionately large and appears to register. The Hallux is short, and Toe 3 relatively long and angled (perhaps with a slight curve) towards the inside of the track (almost 'pigeon-toed'). Talons are quite fine but register in the track.
Similar Species: Similar in size and general shape to the Wood Pigeon. Compare also with Kestrel.

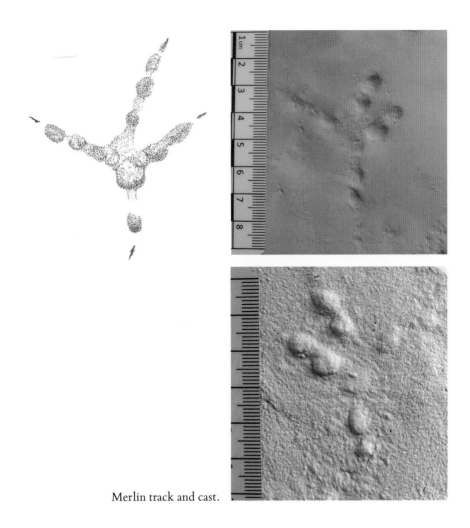

Merlin track and cast.

ZYGODACTYL BIRD TRACKS

Zygodactyl tracks are those that have two toes facing forwards and two toes backwards. This means the Hallux and Toe 4 face backwards, and Toes 2 and 3 face forwards. The biggest group of Zygodactyl species in the British Isles are the Owls, but the Woodpeckers, Parakeets (indeed all Parrots), and Cuckoos all have this foot structure.

OWLS

Track type: Zygodactyl.
Size: Large to Very Large (41–107mm).
Key features: 'K-shaped' track. Hallux much reduced.

SPECIES

Eurasian Eagle-Owl *Bubo bubo*
Tawny Owl *Strix aluco*
Long-eared Owl *Asio otus*
Little Owl *Athene noctua*

Snowy Owl *Bubo scandiacus*
Short-eared Owl *Asio flammeus*
Barn Owl *Tyto alba*

Owls are very similar across the species, and they all have a Zygodactyl foot structure. However, in Owls this is perhaps best described as two toes pointing forwards, one backwards and one sideways (at varying angles). The track describes a 'K shape', with a straight line created by the Hallux and Toe 2 on the inside of the track. The outer Toe 4 may be held backwards, out to the side (coming quite close to 90° and possibly looking a lot like a Marsh Harrier track), or it may also face forwards and therefore show three toes forwards and just one to the back. The three toes forwards pattern is often used in flight, so is unlikely to be found in tracks. However, do keep in mind that Toe 4 can swivel (because of a unique flexible joint) through a range of angles. What is characteristic of Owls, and also commonly occurring species of Woodpeckers, is the very much-reduced Hallux, which and may not actually register very strongly at all. Also check the length of the toes and robustness. For example, Barn Owls have very long, slender toes in comparison with Tawny Owls. There is considerable crossover with some species, especially the medium-sized Owls, and identification in the field may not always be possible. Also keep in mind that size, as with Birds of Prey, may be deceptive because of the sexual dimorphism by size. Female Owls of many species are significantly bigger than the males.

OWL TRACK DESCRIPTIONS

EURASIAN EAGLE-OWL (BUBO BUBO)

Track: 107mm (male). A huge Zygodactyl track with robust toes and long talons. The toes show obvious, separate pads (which register as rough or pitted in good substrates). The track is very broad across the Metatarsal area but the extent to which this registers is dependent on substrate. The Hallux is relatively small (short and narrow), but the pad at its base is large and bulbous.

Similar Species: Only the Snowy Owl potentially overlaps in size (a small male Eagle-Owl is similar in size to a large female Snowy), although Snowy Owl tracks appear to be less robust and are unlikely to be found in the same areas. Compare also with Common Buzzard.

Notes: Tens of pairs of Eagle-Owl are believed to be nesting in northern England, although the origin of these birds is unknown. Male birds are 20 per cent (or more) smaller than the females and this will be reflected to some extent in track lengths.

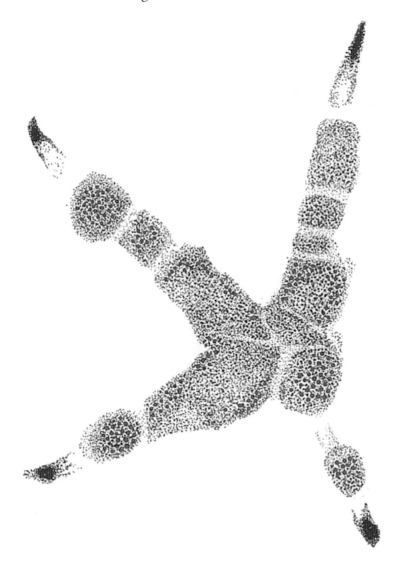

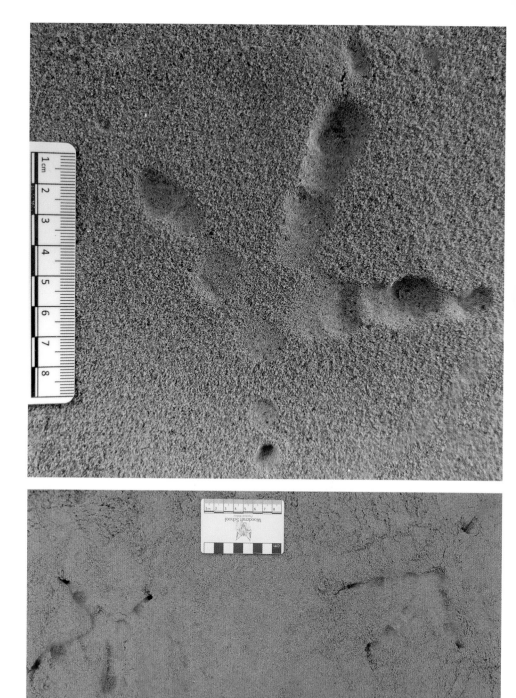

Eurasian Eagle-Owl tracks.

SNOWY OWL (*BUBO SCANDIACUS*)

Track: 85mm. A large Zygodactyl track with robust toes and long talons. The toes show obvious, separate pads. The track is very broad across the Metatarsal area. The Hallux is relatively small (short and narrow).
Similar Species: A small male Eagle-Owl is similar in size to a larger female Snowy, although their tracks will always be more robust.
Notes: A few Snowy Owls turn up in the British Isles each year, and the species used to breed in Shetland (with birds resident there for many years).

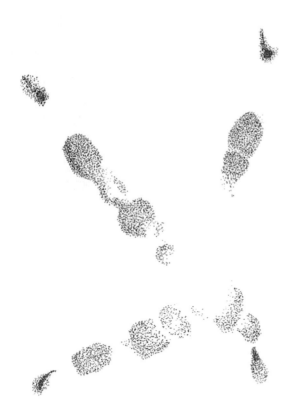

Snowy Owl track and cast. These birds seem to register tracks very lightly.

TAWNY OWL (*STRIX ALUCO*)

Track: 56mm. The most robust of the medium-sized Owl tracks. The toes are relatively short and very bulbous, giving a 'lumpy' shape to the track. Two pads on the inside of the track (at the base of the Hallux and Toe 2) are particularly obvious and make the track look especially broad across the Metatarsal area. The pads appear rough or pitted in good substrates.

Similar Species: Good tracks should be identifiable, but care should be taken separating them from tracks of the 'eared' (*Asio*) Owls, which are similar in size and structure (albeit less robust and a little smaller), and Barn Owl, which is the same size (but much slimmer).

Notes: Tawny Owls visit puddles and ponds in woodlands to bathe and to catch frogs, and we have found their tracks in such situations on a number of occasions.

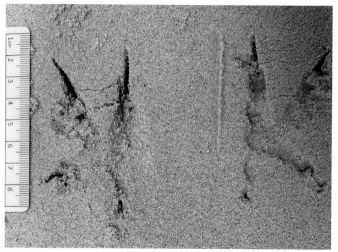

Paired Tawny Owl tracks.

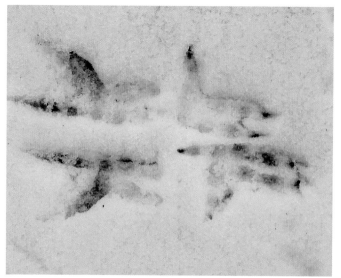

Tawny Owl hopping in snow

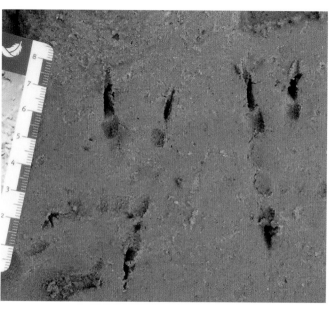

Tawny Owl tracks. (MS)

SHORT-EARED OWL (*ASIO FLAMMEUS*)

Track: 53mm. A classic Zygodactyl Owl track – relatively robust and showing obvious, bulbous toe pads (which appear rough or pitted in good substrates). Two pads on the inside of the track (at the base of the Hallux and Toe 2) are particularly obvious and make the track look broad across the Metatarsal area.

Similar Species: Tawny Owl tracks are similar sized and slightly more robust, although field separation of anything other than the best tracks is probably not possible. Identification based on habitat is probably more reliable. Compare also with Barn Owl, which has less robust (slimmer) tracks and share similar habitats.

Notes: Short-eared Owls are found in open habitats (moorland, heathland, meadows and fens) and sit on the ground regularly, although we have not found their tracks.

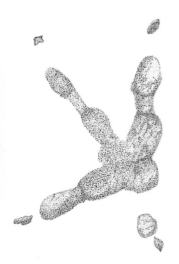

Short-eared Owl track and cast.

LONG-EARED OWL (*ASIO OTUS*)

Track: 50mm. A classic Zygodactyl Owl track. The smallest of the medium-sized Owl tracks. Relatively robust with obvious, bulbous toe pads.
Similar Species: Tawny Owl tracks are larger, more robust and the toe pads more obviously bulbous. The Short-eared Owl is very similar (slightly more robust), and the Barn Owl has long, slender toes.

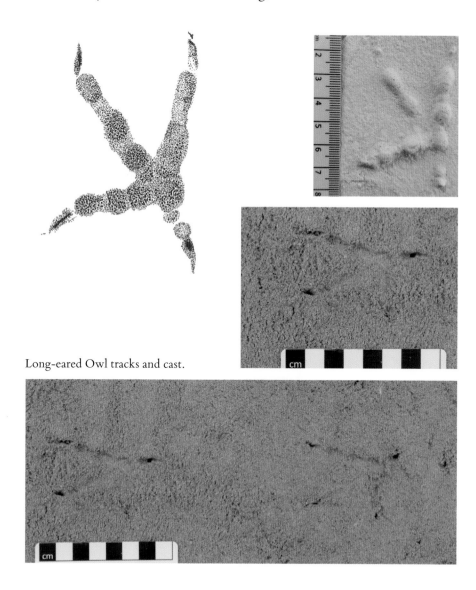

Long-eared Owl tracks and cast.

BARN OWL (*TYTO ALBA*)

Track: 55mm. A classic Zygodactyl Owl track but with relatively long, slim toes. The toes do show clear, bulbous pads, but these are less prominent than in the other Owl species.

Similar Species: Tawny Owl tracks are the same size but are significantly more robust, with the prominent pads giving them a lumpy appearance (in comparison to the long, relatively slender toes of Barn Owl). Barn Owls are a little smaller (10 per cent) and lighter than Tawny Owls. Compare also with the 'eared' (*Asio*) Owls.

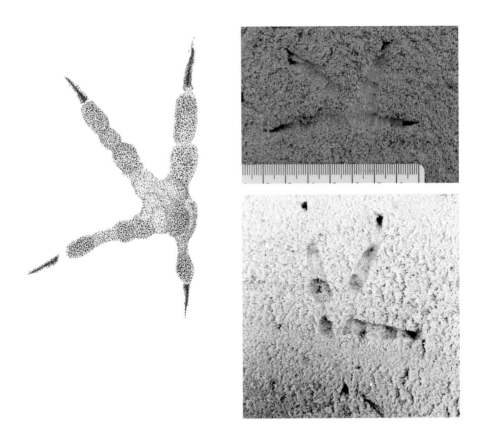

Barn Owl tracks.

LITTLE OWL (*ATHENE NOCTUA*)

Track: 41mm. A classic but tiny Zygodactyl Owl track with robust toes that show obvious bulbous pads (including the pads at the ends of the toes), which register as rough or pitted in good substrates. The talons show in the tracks.

Similar Species: The tracks of other Owl species are all significantly larger. The bulbous pads at the ends of the toes also seem to be diagnostic. See also Woodpecker tracks, which are similar in size. Woodpeckers, however, have much slimmer toes, a very short Hallux and Toe 4 points directly backwards, forming (more or less) a straight line with Toe 3.

Notes: Little Owls forage for food on the ground, so will leave tracks in the right situation.

Right and below: Little Owl track and cast.

Below left: Little Owl tracks. (MS)

WOODPECKERS AND PARAKEET

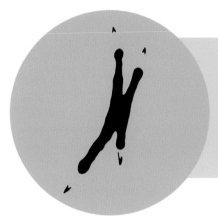

Track type: Zygodactyl.
Size: Small to Medium (34–47mm).
Key features: Two toes forwards, two back. Toes 3 and 4 form a straight line on the outside of the track. Hallux small and registers weakly.

SPECIES

Green Woodpecker *Picus viridis*
Great Spotted Woodpecker *Dendrocopos major*
Rose-ringed Parakeet *Psittacula krameri*

Woodpeckers all have Zygodactyl feet, with Toes 3 and 4 forming a straight line on the outside of the track (in contrast to Owls). We haven't managed to find and isolate the tracks of our smallest species, the Lesser Spotted Woodpecker, but based on measurements of museum specimens it has a similarly proportioned foot but is tiny at just *c*.25mm long. Similarly, the Eurasian Wryneck, now a passage migrant in Britain, has the same foot structure. Like the Owls, Woodpeckers consistently show two toes facing forward and two back. The Hallux is small and weak-looking in Woodpeckers, and may not register. Woodpeckers hop, so look for side-by-side tracks. Parakeets are similar, but the Hallux tends to register more strongly than in Woodpeckers. The Wryneck is a small species of woodpecker that is also worth considering when identifying tracks. They are very rare visitors to the UK but may still be encountered. The likelihood of finding them would increase in mainland Europe.

Green Woodpecker in the hand, showing off its Zygodactyl feet.

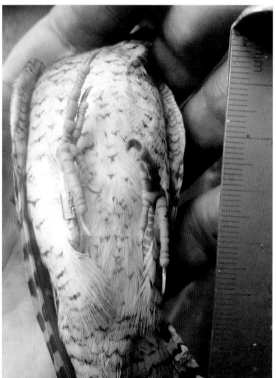

Wryneck in the hand, showing its Woodpecker feet.

WOODPECKERS AND PARAKEET TRACK DESCRIPTIONS

GREEN WOODPECKER (*PICUS VIRIDIS*)

Track: 46mm. Classic Zygodactyl foot with Toes 2 and 3 pointing forwards, and the Hallux and Toe 4 backwards. Toes 3 and 4 are the longest and form a straight line on the outside of the track. The Hallux is very small (*c.*5mm), but seems to register in the track, as do the nails. The Metatarsal area also registers.

Similar Species: Great Spotted Woodpecker is smaller with a proportionately longer Hallux. Little Owl is a similar size but with bulbous pads on robust toes, and Toes 3 and 4 are not held in a straight line.

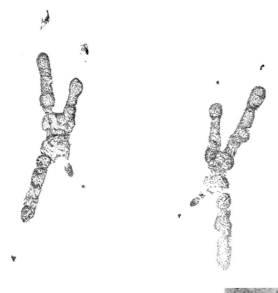

Green Woodpecker tracks.

GREAT SPOTTED WOODPECKER
(*DENDROCOPUS MAJOR*)

Track: 34mm. Classic Zygodactyl foot with Toes 2 and 3 pointing forwards, and the Hallux and Toe 4 backwards. Toes 3 and 4 are the longest and form a straight line on the outside of the track. The Hallux is small but seems to register in the track, as do the nails. The Metatarsal area also registers.

Similar Species: Green Woodpecker is larger with a proportionately shorter Hallux.

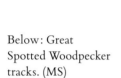

Below: Great
Spotted Woodpecker
tracks. (MS)

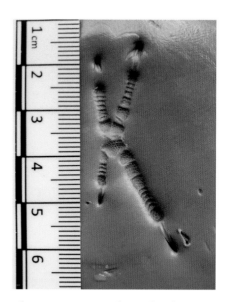

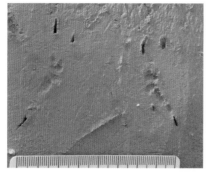

Above: Great Spotted Woodpecker
foot impression in clay.

Left: Great Spotted Woodpecker
tracks in clay.

184

ROSE-RINGED PARAKEET (*PSITTACULA KRAMERI*)

Track: 47mm. Classic Zygodactyl foot with Toes 2 and 3 pointing forwards, and the Hallux and Toe 4 backwards. Toes 3 and 4 are the longest. The forward-facing toes hug very close together whereas the Hallux and Toe 4 are splayed, making the track look like an inverted capital 'Y'. The Metatarsal registers weakly, but the long nails appear to register reliably.
Similar Species: Compare the overall track shape (and proportions) with the Woodpeckers and Little Owl.
Notes: Drawn from track and foot photos in Nauta and Pot (2019). This species is common in and around Greater London, with the population expanding northwards.

Rose-ringed Parakeet track. (RN)

GAMEBIRD TRACKS

Track type: Classic.
Size: Medium to Very Large (34–47mm).
Key features: Hallux greatly reduced.
Robust toes. Obvious Metatarsal pad.

As a group, these birds spend the majority of their time on the ground, and this has influenced their foot morphology. They have classic, Anisodactyl feet, but the Hallux is greatly reduced and therefore may not show in the track, show weakly, or only occasionally show. When it does show, it points to the centre of the trail and often forms a straight line with Toe 4. The toes in this group are robust, and the tips of Toes 2 and/or 4 tend to dip (or droop) down towards the bottom of the track. The Metatarsal area, as is true with many birds that walk a good deal, frequently registers strongly. A number of species have proximal webbing between Toes 2 and 3, and Toes 3 and 4, which may or may not show in the tracks (depending on substrate). The Gamebirds range in size from the enormous Great Bustard to smaller species such as Partridges and Quail.

The largest – the Great Bustard – is rare to encounter in the wild but the species is being re-established as a breeding bird (see below), so we have included it here. We have also included some domestic fowl that will, like the ornamental Indian Peafowl, most often be encountered close to farms and human habitation.

SPECIES

Great Bustard *Otis tarda*
Capercaillie *Tetrao urogallus*
Domestic Turkey *Meleagris gallopavo domesticus*
Indian Peafowl *Pavo cristatus*
Chicken *Gallus gallus*
Domestic Guineafowl *Numida meleagris domestica*
Pheasant *Phasianus colchicus*
Black Grouse *Lyrurus tetrix*
Red Grouse *Lagopus lagopus*
Red-legged Partridge *Alectoris rufa*
Grey Partridge *Perdix perdix*
Common Quail *Coturnix coturnix*

VERY LARGE GAMEBIRD TRACKS

Great Bustards have extremely large tracks, as would be expected from the world's heaviest flying bird. Their toes are fat and bulbous, which coupled with their size makes the track unmistakable. Great Bustards were reintroduced to England in 2004 (having become extinct in the 1830s), with about 100 birds now established and breeding annually on Salisbury Plain in Wiltshire. Standing at around 1m tall, with a wingspan of 2–2.5m and weighing over 10kg, the Great Bustard is one of the largest extant flying animals.

Where they occur together, the most likely confusion species are White Stork and Common Crane. However, check the angle of the outer toe – Toe 4 – to separate these species. In the case of the Common Crane it is set close to 90° from the central Toe 3.

The Capercaillie is the largest member of the Grouse family and can be differentiated from the large domesticated Gamebirds by the fringes ('snow shoes') around Toes 2, 3 and 4. It is a rare resident of northern Scotland, preferring large tracts of mature coniferous forest, and tending to avoid open ground.

LARGE GAMEBIRD TRACKS

The large Gamebirds include Red and Black Grouse, and the introduced – and in some regions the very common – Pheasant. Other similar-sized species that may be confused are all domesticated and include Chickens, Peacocks and Turkeys. Guineafowl are also quite common in some regions, and with the exception of the Pheasant, are likely to be the largest non-native Gamebird tracks most often encountered far from habitation. Chickens will tend to be closely associated with humans, and keep in mind that they vary in size from the diminutive Bantams to the much larger 'Black Rock' breeds and this size difference will be reflected in the tracks.

Black Grouse are rare residents of northern uplands, where they prefer woodland edge on moorland or heathland, or lake shores. In contrast, Red Grouse are common on and adjacent to moorland in the uplands, especially those moors managed for the sport shooting of this species. Pheasant tracks are one of the most commonly found bird tracks in the British Isles (unsurprisingly, with over 35 million individuals released for sport shooting each year). There is considerable size variation between the various breeds being released, which will almost certainly show in the tracks.

MEDIUM GAMEBIRD TRACKS

Our two Partridge species – the introduced Red-legged Partridge and our native Grey Partridge – are indistinguishable in the field from their tracks. Both species have tracks that look very similar to a small version of a Pheasant track. They are most often encountered in open areas, especially arable fields, and frequently in small groups (or coveys).

Common Quail are close in size to Partridges but have much more delicate toes. They are rarely seen, keeping well hidden in pasture and farmland, so keep this in mind when considering track identification. Tracks in the open will most likely to belong to Partridges. An increasingly rare migrant breeder in the British Isles but more common across the rest of Europe.

GAMEBIRD TRACK DESCRIPTIONS

GREAT BUSTARD (*OTIS TARDA*)

Track: 100mm. A huge, unique track comprising three fleshy toes. Toe 2 is the shortest, and Toe 3 the longest. Toes 2 and 4 point more forwards than in the tracks of other similar-sized species. The nails register as continuous from the end of the toes, tapering to a point. The nail on Toe 2 may not register in harder substrates, making this digit look even shorter. The Metatarsal pad registers reliably, is large and circular. There is no Hallux.
Similar Species: The larger Herons, Common Crane and White Stork have similar-sized tracks but are structurally quite different (slender toes, and with a Hallux).

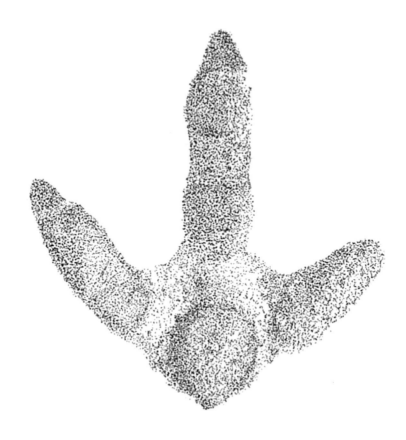

The dinosaur-like feet of the
Great Bustard. (GS)

Below: Great Bustard tracks.
(MK)

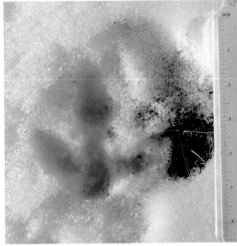

CAPERCAILLIE *(TETRAO UROGALLUS)*

Track: 88mm. A very large, typical Gamebird track. Robust toes, with Toe 3 relatively short compared to other Gamebirds. The Hallux registers reliably, as does the large Metatarsal pad. Nails leave clear, rounded marks. In winter the toes are fringed with long, comb-like bristles, making the impression of each toe much wider. These bristles are a snow shoe adaptation. The tracks of male birds are a third larger than those of the hen.

Similar Species: Black Grouse tracks are significantly smaller and likely to be found in more open areas.

Capercaillie tracks in the snow.

DOMESTIC TURKEY
(*MELEAGRIS GALLOPAVO DOMESTICUS*)

Track: 89mm. A very large track with robust, tapering toes, bulbous toe pads and broad nails. The Hallux is long and tends to register reliably, as does the large Metatarsal pad.

Similar Species: Other large domesticated Gamebirds such as Indian Peafowl. In appropriate habitat, consider also the White Stork and Common Crane. Male Turkeys can be twice as heavy as females, which is reflected in the size of their tracks.

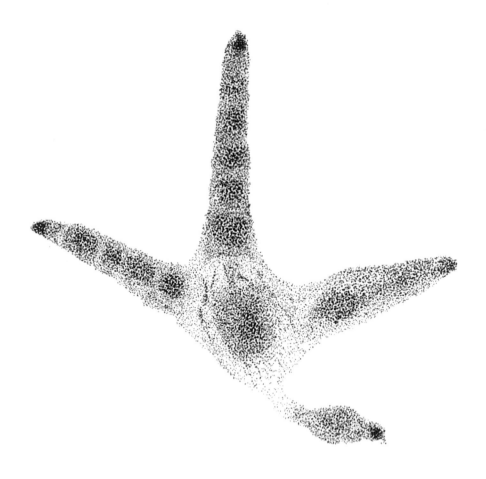

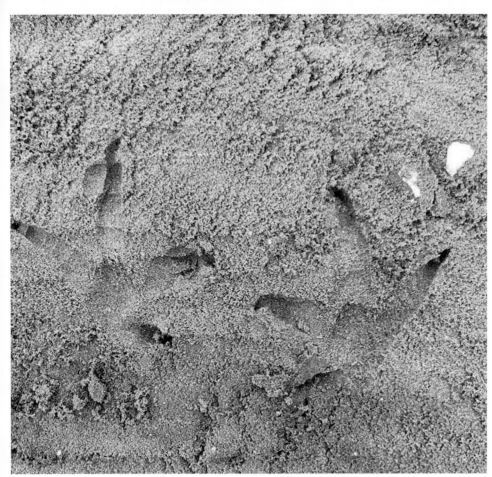

Domestic Turkey
track. (GC)

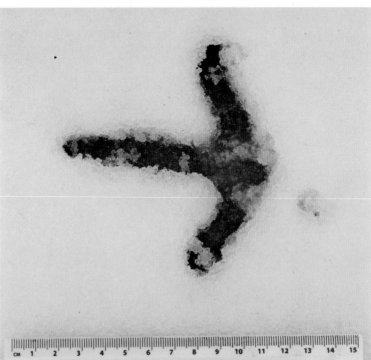

Wild Turkey
(*Meleagris gallopavo*)
track in the snow.

INDIAN PEAFOWL/PEACOCK (*PAVO CRISTATUS*)

Track: 87mm. Very large with robust toes. Toe 3 is long and straight. Toe 4 is thinner and appears to be bent downwards towards the tip. Toe 2 is distinctly shorter. Long nails register reliably, as does the large Metatarsal pad. The Hallux is long and registers often.

Similar Species: Size alone rules out most other similar species other than the Domestic Turkey, which has more robust, tapering toes (see also that species).

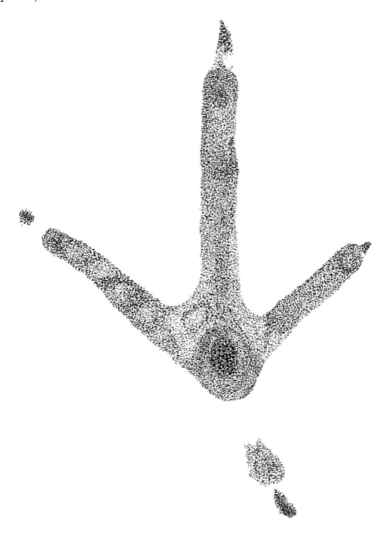

Indian Peafowl (Peacock)
tracks. (MSr)

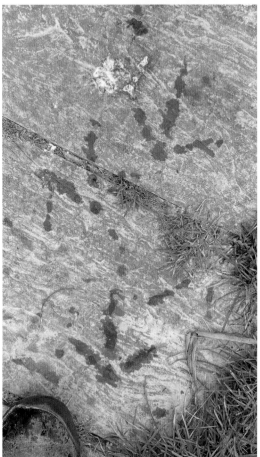

CHICKEN (*GALLUS GALLUS*)

Track: 63mm. Relatively robust Toes, with Toes 2 and 4 similar in length. Nails are long and show reliably in the tracks, with those on Toes 2 and 4 curving downwards, which emphasizes the slightly down-curved toes (giving a 'drooping' look to them). The Hallux is long and shows reliably, as does the large Metatarsal pad.

Similar Species: Similar to the Pheasant (where size overlaps: see Notes) although Pheasant has more slender toes, and Toe 2 is noticeably the shortest. The Hallux in the Chicken is longer and larger. Compare also with the smaller Domestic Guineafowl.

Notes: The numerous different Chicken breeds vary dramatically in size, so the variation in track size will also be significant.

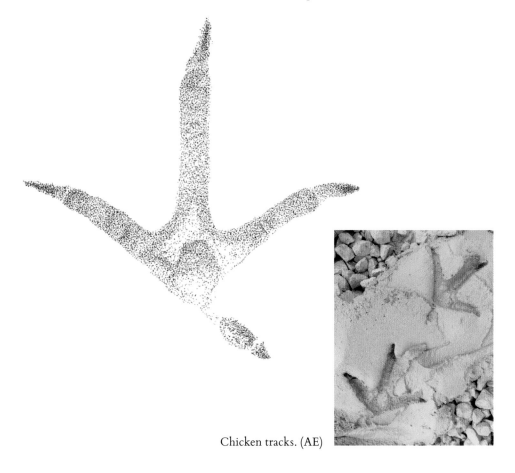

Chicken tracks. (AE)

DOMESTIC GUINEAFOWL
(*NUMIDA MELEAGRIS DOMESTICA*)

Track: 55mm. Robust toes, with Toe 2 noticeably shorter than Toe 4. Nails are long and show reliably in the tracks, with those on Toes 2 and 4 curving downwards, which emphasizes the slightly down-curved toes (giving a 'drooping' look to them). The Hallux is long and shows reliably, as does the large Metatarsal pad.

Similar Species: Similar to the Pheasant, although Pheasant has more slender, more droopy toes (Toes 2 and 4) and shorter nails. Pheasants also tend to have Toes 2 and 4 held slightly lower. Compare also with Chicken.

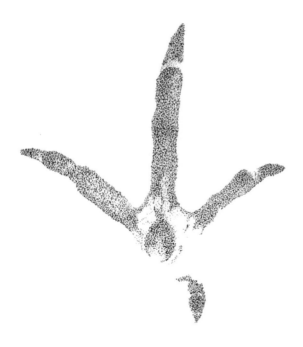

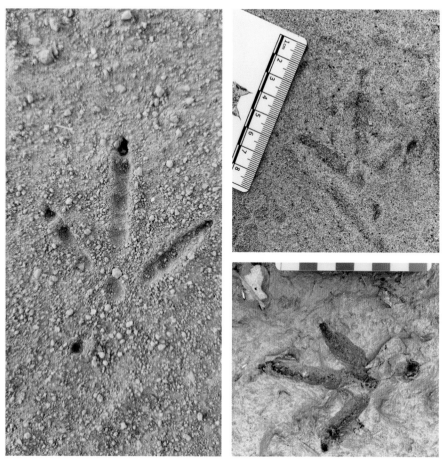

Clockwise from above: Helmeted Guineafowl (*Numida meleagris*) track (AN); Helmeted Guineafowl track (RB); Domestic Guineafowl track in soft mud.

PHEASANT (*PHASIANUS COLCHICUS*)

Track: 55mm. Toes relatively slender and clearly of uneven lengths. Toe 3 is long and straight and often showing distinct individual segments (or pads). Toe 4 is thinner and often appears to be bent downwards towards the tip. Toe 2 is distinctly shorter. Large, pointed nails register reliably, as does the large Metatarsal pad (at least in slower-moving birds). The Hallux registers often but by no means always. In good substrates, proximal webbing between the toes may be seen.

Similar Species: Partridge tracks are smaller and the nails less often visible. Red Grouse tracks are smaller and the toes are more robust and proportionately shorter. Black Grouse tracks are similar in size but have more robust toes (and Toe 4 is shorter). Domestic Guineafowl are very similar but with more robust toes and longer nails, and Toes 2 and 4 held slightly higher.

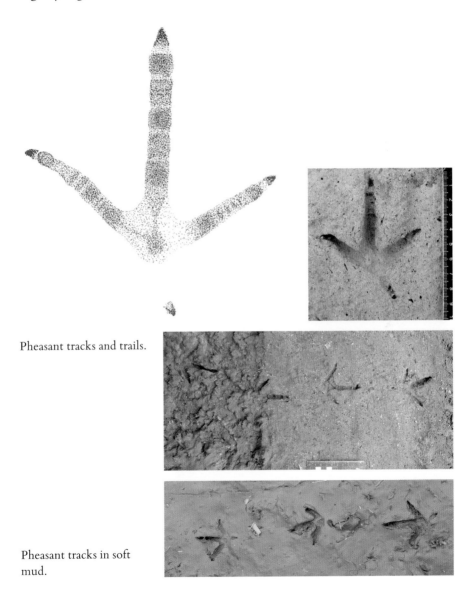

Pheasant tracks and trails.

Pheasant tracks in soft mud.

BLACK GROUSE (*LYRURUS TETRIX*)

Track: 53mm. A typical Gamebird track with robust toes. The rounded nails register reliably, as does the Metatarsal pad and Hallux. Black Grouse have fringed toes like Capercaillie, which will show in the tracks, especially so in the winter. Male Black Grouse are significantly larger than the hens.
Similar Species: Structurally similar to the Capercaillie but smaller, and more robust, and larger than the Red Grouse. Both of these species tend to prefer different habitats to Black Grouse (see Introduction).

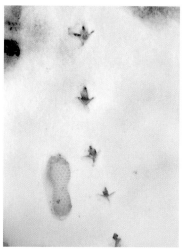

Top right: Black Grouse trail in snow showing how substrate can distort tracks. (LS)

Bottom right: Black Grouse in snow. (DP)

RED GROUSE (*LAGOPUS LAGOPUS*)

Track: 41mm. A classic Gamebird track with slender toes. The Hallux is long and registers quite reliably, as does the Metatarsal pad. Both Toes 2 and 4 bend downwards (droop) at the tip. Proximal webbing between the toes may be seen in good substrates. Robust, rounded nails. The toes are feathered in winter, which can lead to less distinct, poorly defined tracks (which itself is an identification feature).

Similar Species: While track size is similar to those of Partridges, Red Grouse toes are more robust (and parallel-sided), have larger nails and Toes 2 and 4 are held at greater angles to Toe 3 than in Partridges. Pheasant tracks are larger.

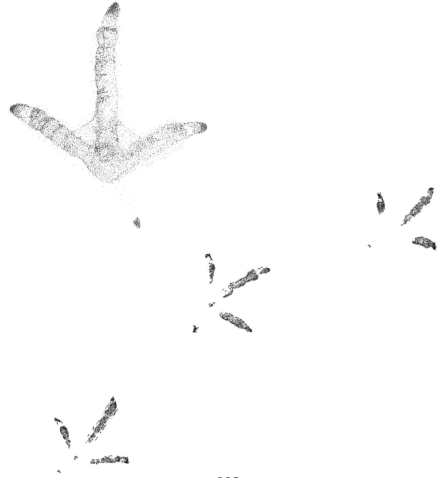

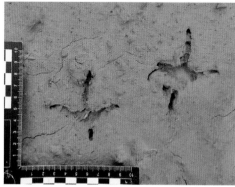

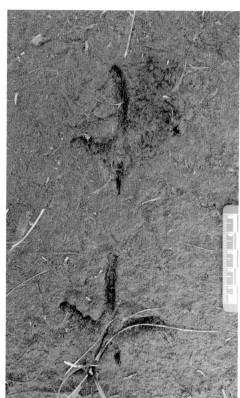

Top left: Red Grouse track.

Other images: Red Grouse tracks and trails.

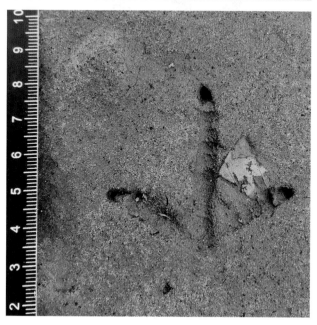

RED-LEGGED PARTRIDGE (*ALECTORIS RUFA*)

Track: 42mm. Slender, tapering toes with Toe 3 relatively long (which can create the impression of a narrow track). Nail marks are relatively fine. The Hallux is small and doesn't always register in the track. The Metatarsal pad registers clearly and reliably. Proximal webbing is present between the toes and may be noticeable in good substrates.

Similar Species: Seemingly identical to the Grey Partridge and unlikely to be separable in the field. Noticeably smaller than Pheasant.

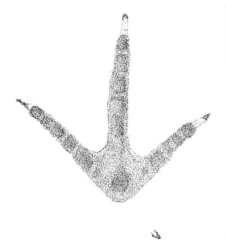

Red-legged Partridge tracks.

GREY PARTRIDGE (*PERDIX PERDIX*)

Track: 42mm. Slender, tapering toes with Toe 3 relatively long (which can create the impression of a narrow track). Nail marks are relatively fine. The Hallux is small and doesn't always register in the track. The Metatarsal pad registers clearly and reliably.
Similar Species: Seemingly identical to Red-legged Partridge and unlikely to be separable in the field. Noticeably smaller than the Pheasant.

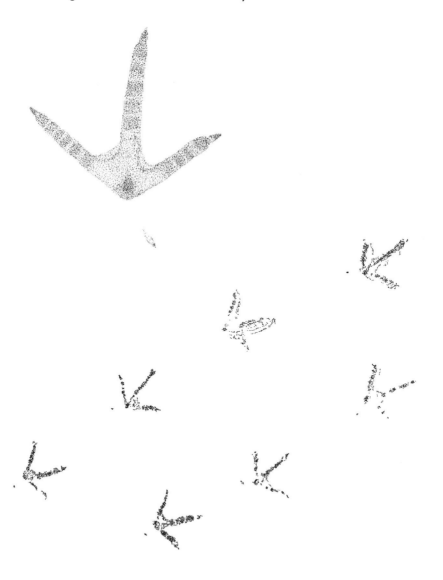

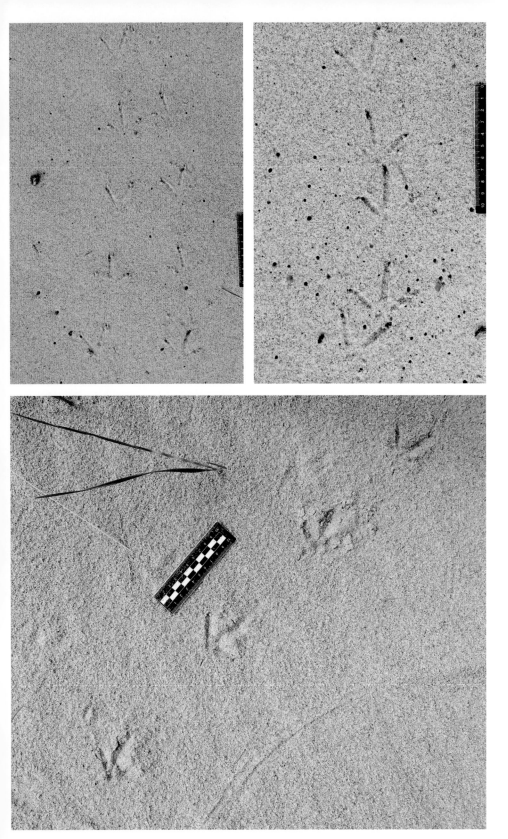

Grey Partridge tracks and trails.

COMMON QUAIL (*COTURNIX COTURNIX*)

Track: 39mm. Small, with delicate toes compared to the other Gamebirds. Toe 1 is narrow and sometimes doesn't register (Grolms, 2021). The Metatarsal pad registers reliably. Nail marks are small and narrow.

Similar Species: A little smaller and with finer, more slender toes than Partridge tracks. Tracks potentially confusable with Wader species such as the Lapwing.

Notes: The track illustrated here was drawn from a photo in van Diepenbeek (2019), foot impressions in Bergmann and Klaus (2016), and checked against drawings in Abenza (2018).

WADER TRACKS

Track type: Classic.
Size: Small to Very Large (19–50mm).
Key features: Hallux greatly reduced and may be absent. Slender toes. Variable proximal webbing.

Waders (or Shorebirds in North America) have a very similar foot structure to Gamebirds, but their toes are proportionately more slender when compared to the former. As a group they have three toes facing forwards and a reduced Hallux backwards. The Hallux is the big variable across the group in that it may register very weakly, quite strongly, or in some species may be physically absent entirely. Many of the Waders have partial (proximal) webbing between one or both forwards-facing toes and Toe 3, presumably as an adaptation to walking across wet mud. The tendency is for this to be present between Toes 3 and 4, but if also present between Toes 2 and 3, the outermost web will be the largest. Whether or not this is seen in the track will depend on the substrate. Most often, if the track is asymmetrical it will be Toe 4 that is held the closer to Toe 3.

Wader tracks may be confused with those of Web-footed birds, mostly because in the latter, the web (in some substrates) may not show. However, Waders have very straight Toes 2 and 4 with no evidence of the curve that is very often seen in the toes of Web-footed bird tracks. Confusion with Gamebirds is possible, but Wader toes are slender by comparison, at least in the most frequently encountered species.

We have grouped the Wader tracks from a tracking perspective, based on general size, toe angles and presence and absence of the Hallux and the Metatarsal area, rather than their biological relationships (although we have also tried to keep this in mind). These divisions are difficult and there are inevitable crossovers, but we think this works best when faced with an unidentified track in the field.

SPECIES

Eurasian Curlew *Numenius arquata*
Whimbrel *Numenius phaeopus*
Black-tailed Godwit *Limosa limosa*
Bar-tailed Godwit *Limosa lapponica*
Oystercatcher *Haematopus ostralegus*
Pied Avocet *Recurvirostra avosetta*
Black-winged Stilt *Himantopus himantopus*
Stone-curlew *Burhinus oedicnemus*

Grey Plover *Pluvialis squatarola*
Golden Plover *Pluvialis apricaria*
Lapwing *Vanellus vanellus*
Redshank *Tringa totanus*
Green Sandpiper *Tringa ochropus*

Turnstone *Arenaria interpres*
Common Sandpiper *Actitis hypoleucos*
Dunlin *Calidris alpina*
Ringed Plover *Charadrius hiaticula*
Little Ringed Plover *Charadrius dubius*
Sanderling *Calidris alba*

Woodcock *Scolopax rusticola*
Common Snipe *Gallinago gallinago*
Jack Snipe *Lymnocryptes minimus*

LARGE WADER TRACKS

The largest Wader tracks range in size from about 39mm to 50mm. The most commonly found tracks are those of Curlew and Oystercatcher. The Curlew (and the similar but smaller Whimbrel) characteristically has the outer Toe 4 held very close to 90° from the central Toe 3, which is itself very straight and forward facing. The inner Toe 2, if anything, maybe be set slightly lower in the track than Toe 4, and is also slightly shorter than Toe 4, although this can be difficult to see. The Hallux is frequently present, even if it is just as a dot, and the Metatarsal registers quite strongly. Very similar to the Curlew (and Whimbrel) tracks are those of the Godwits, which also hold Toes 2 and 4 quite close to 90°. However, Godwits have a very faintly registering Metatarsal area and their Hallux registers more strongly. Additionally, the inner Toe 2 is noticeably shorter than Toe 4. The Curlew is a common track on sandy beaches and coastal mudflats and estuaries, which are also favoured by Oystercatchers, so familiarisation with the tracks of these two species is a good starting point for the coastal tracker. Oystercatcher tracks are also quite large and their Toes 2 and 4 can appear really quite close to 90° from Toe 3. The tracks are incredibly varied and can look like they have very fat toes (their toes are very fat), or can appear quite slender when partially registering on harder substrates. They have obvious (partial) webbing between Toes 3 and 4, which makes the outside of the track look 'fat'. Other large Waders included in this group are all unique and include the highly asymmetrical and webbed Avocet, the slender-toed and 'webbed on one side' Black-winged Stilt, and the fleshy forward-facing toes of the Stone-curlew (which is a dry, sandy substrate Wader).

MEDIUM TO SMALL WADERS WITH HALLUX REGISTERING

This group comprises Wader tracks with relatively slender, often spear-shaped toes, ranging in size from 23 to 33mm long and (importantly) reliably registering a Hallux. Included here are the *Tringa* 'shanks' and Sandpipers, but also a Plover (Lapwing), Dunlin and Turnstone. Do be careful, though, when making an analysis based on the presence or absence of the Hallux. Even with species that possess this feature it may not be obvious dependent on substrate.

MEDIUM TO SMALL WADER TRACKS WITH NO HALLUX

This group comprises the tracks of various Plover species but also the minute tracks of the Sanderling, all of which have relatively slender, often spear-shaped toes, ranging in size from 19 to 35mm long and (importantly) have no Hallux to register. The Metatarsal area registers weakly, if at all.

MEDIUM, SLENDER-TOED WADER TRACKS

All three Snipe species – Woodcock, Snipe and Jack Snipe – have a very similar foot structure, and are all found in wet habitats such as marshes, wetlands, coastal salt-marsh and wet heaths. Woodcock also frequent and nest in damp woodlands. The fact that these species are frequently encountered in wet meadows and fields means their tracks could be confused with Gamebirds. Their tracks have long, slender toes, a Hallux that registers often and a round dot of a Metatarsal pad. The Jack Snipe is obviously the smallest at 28mm, but the Snipe and Woodcock are more similar in size (34 and 39mm respectively), and may not be reliably distinguished in the field. Woodcock is slightly larger with more robust toes, and the Metatarsal area is proportionately broader, which seems to the be the most reliable feature to separate the species, but this can be quite subjective depending on the quality of the track.

WADER TRACK DESCRIPTIONS

EURASIAN CURLEW *(NUMENIUS ARQUATA)*

Track: 50mm. Our largest Wader track. Three robust, spear-shaped toes. Toes 2 and 4 are angled far back, making the track look very wide. Toe 4 is longer than Toe 2. Partial webbing is present between Toes 3 and 4, and to a lesser extent between Toes 3 and 2. The Hallux is set significantly behind the Metatarsal area and shows reliably in tracks. The Metatarsal pad only shows in deeper substrates.

Similar species: Whimbrel tracks are almost identical, but smaller (although there may be overlap). Black-tailed Godwit tracks appear less robust than the Eurasian Curlew. Oystercatcher tracks are smaller, the toes less tapering (fleshier), and Toes 2 and 4 are angled further forwards than in Eurasian Curlew.

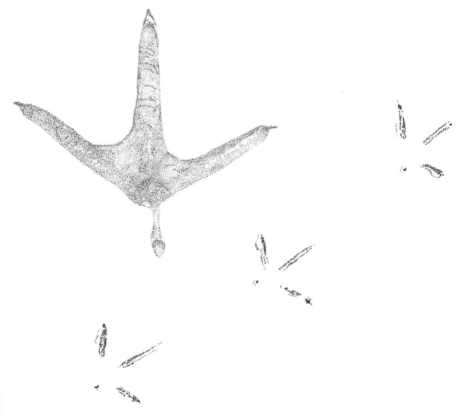

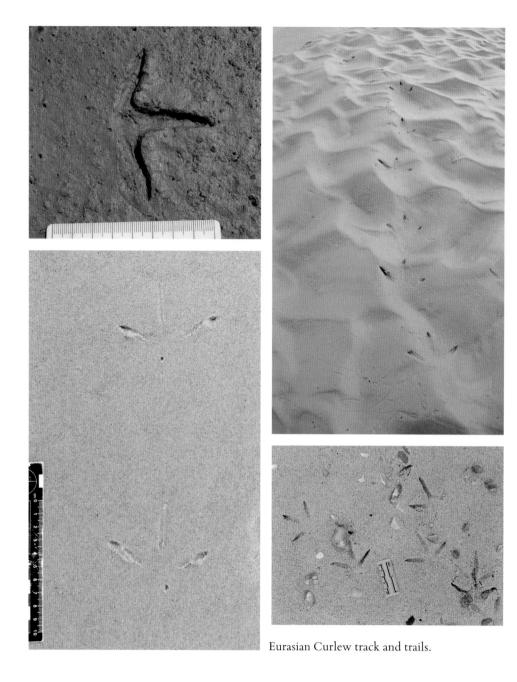

Eurasian Curlew track and trails.

WHIMBREL (*NUMENIUS PHAEOPUS*)

Track: 45mm. Large with three robust, spear-shaped toes. Toes 2 and 4 are angled far back, making the track very wide. Toe 4 is longer than Toe 2. Partial webbing is present between Toes 3 and 4, and to a lesser extent between Toes 3 and 2. The Hallux is set significantly behind the Metatarsal area and shows reliably in tracks. The Metatarsal pad only shows in deeper substrates.

Similar species: Eurasian Curlew tracks are almost identical, but larger (although there may be overlap). Black-tailed Godwit tracks appear less robust, but are otherwise very similar. Oystercatcher tracks show fleshier, less tapering toes, and Toes 2 and 4 are angled further forwards than in Whimbrel.

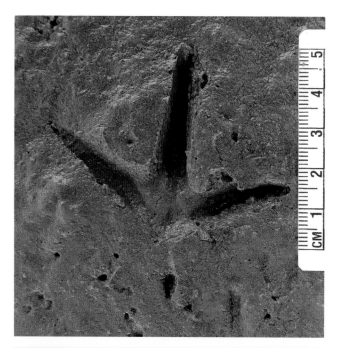

Whimbrel tracks in estuary mud.

BLACK-TAILED GODWIT (*LIMOSA LIMOSA*)

Track: 47mm. Large with three relatively robust, spear-shaped toes and partial webbing between Toes 3 and 4. The Hallux is long and appears to show well in tracks, whereas the Metatarsal pad registers weakly except in softer substrates.

Similar Species: Perhaps most similar to Whimbrel tracks, which are a little more robust. Eurasian Curlew tracks are slightly larger, wider and with more robust toes. Compare also with the smaller Bar-tailed Godwit.

Notes: Based on the trail of just one individual.

Black-tailed Godwit track.

BAR-TAILED GODWIT (*LIMOSA LAPPONICA*)

Track: 40mm. Three relatively robust, spear-shaped toes and partial webbing between Toes 3 and 4. The Hallux is long and shows reliably in tracks, whereas the Metatarsal pad registers weakly, if at all, except in softer substrates.
Similar Species: Whimbrel tracks are larger and a little more robust. Compare also with the larger Black-tailed Godwit.

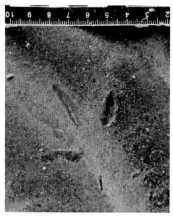

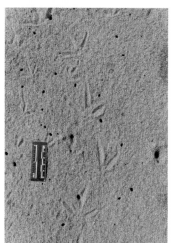

Note the large Metatarsal negative space in these Bar-tailed Godwit tracks.

OYSTERCATCHER (*HAEMATOPUS OSTRALEGUS*)

Track: 44mm. Three fleshy, robust and spear-shaped toes. No Hallux. The track is wider than it is long. Toe 4 is longer than Toe 2, and is set slightly but noticeably further back. The Metatarsal pad registers regularly, sometimes as a 'heel' that extends behind the toes. Partial webbing between Toes 3 and 4 is obvious in softer substrates.

Similar Species: The Eurasian Curlew is larger (especially wider), with Toes 2 and 4 set further back.

Notes: Found regularly on a range of substrates (hard and soft sand, dry sand, and hard and soft mud), so the tracks can present in a variety of forms, although track size and angles between the toes are almost always diagnostic.

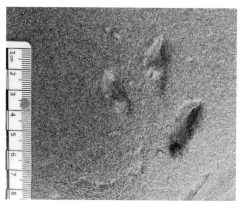

Above: Oystercatcher track with the toes all close together (probably running).

Other images: Oystercatcher tracks and trails in a variety of substrates.

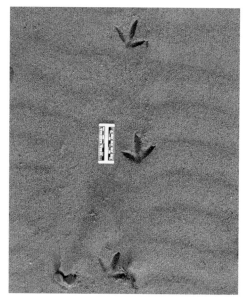

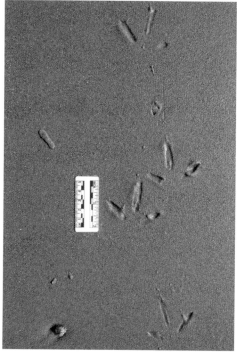

PIED AVOCET (*RECURVIROSTRA AVOSETTA*)

Track: Approx. 42mm. A unique Wader track with toes all obviously different lengths (Toe 2 clearly the shortest). Toes 2 and 4 are curved inwards. Webbing is present between each of the toes, but is asymmetrical (due to the different toe lengths). The Metatarsal pad is small but shows in the track. A tiny Hallux (about 2mm long) is present but is set quite far up the leg and would only register in deep mud.

Similar Species: Compare with other webbed species such as similar-sized Gulls.

Notes: Drawn from track photos of American Avocet (*Recurvirostra americana*) in Elbroch and Marks (2001) and Nauta and Pot (2019). Comparison of museum skins of both the American and Pied Avocets confirm that the foot structure is identical and foot size approximately the same. Track length is approximate as we have been unable to measure the actual tracks of Pied Avocet.

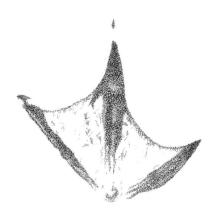

BLACK-WINGED STILT (*HIMANTOPUS HIMANTOPUS*)

Track: 40mm. Long, slender toes, with Toe 3 noticeably the longest (the other two are similar in lengths). No Hallux. The Metatarsal pad is small but shows regularly in the tracks. Significant webbing is present between Toes 3 and 4, with just a small web between the other toes (which may not be obvious in the track).

Similar Species: No other species has this combination of size, slender toes and webbing.

Notes: Drawn from a photo of two tracks in Abenza García (2018). Size also as published in Abenza García (2018) and confirmed against museum specimens.

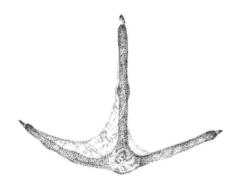

STONE-CURLEW (*BURHINUS OEDICNEMUS*)

Track: 39mm. A unique track of three fleshy, robust, forward-facing toes that are rounded at the ends. No Hallux. The Metatarsal pad registers reliably as a small circular spot. Toe 2 is shorter, thinner and held closer to Toe 3 than is Toe 4. There is partial webbing between Toes 3 and 4. Nails show reliably, especially so on Toe 3, where it can be indistinguishable from the end of the toe (particularly in sandy and dusty substrates).

Similar Species: Not like any other bird of this size in the British Isles – the track morphology is immediately diagnostic in the field. Great Bustard has an almost identical foot structure and consequently its tracks look like giant Stone-curlew tracks.

Notes: Stone-curlews inhabit dry, sandy areas and can leave long trails in suitable substrates when actively feeding at night. A typical trail is illustrated, but it is worth noting that the feet can cross over onto the opposite ('wrong') side of the trail (especially when reaching for an insect). Look for the shorter, hugging Toe 2 to determine left from right.

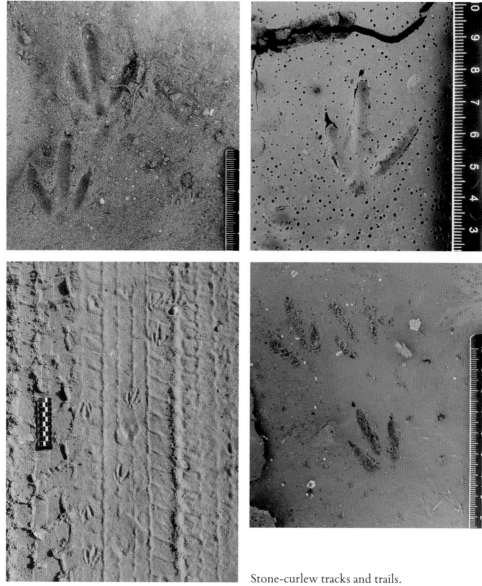

Stone-curlew tracks and trails.

GREY PLOVER (*PLUVIALIS SQUATAROLA*)

Track: 35mm. Three spear-shaped toes. No Hallux. Tracks are asymmetrical with toes all slightly different lengths and Toe 4 angled closer to the central Toe 3 than is Toe 2. The Metatarsal area registers weakly, if at all, except in softer substrates when the partial webbing between Toes 3 and 4 can also show.

Similar Species: Difficult to distinguish from Golden Plover tracks, which are, however, slightly smaller and less robust. Lapwing tracks are also smaller, less robust but show a Hallux in good substrate.

Notes: Grey Plovers are primarily coastal birds (on migration and in winter), and prefer sandy beaches and muddy estuaries, which are less commonly used by the other species that leave similar tracks.

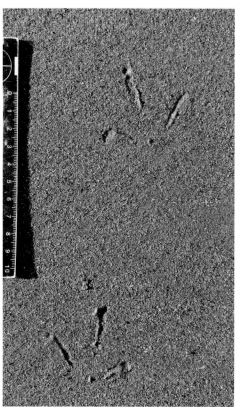
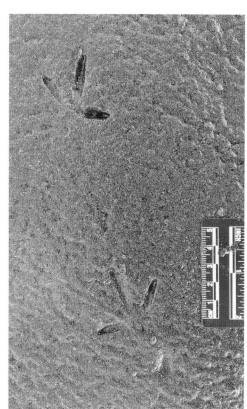

Grey Plover tracks.

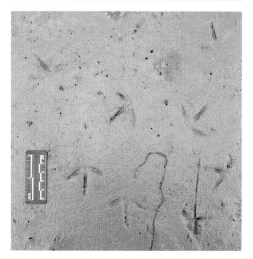

GOLDEN PLOVER (*PLUVIALIS APRICARIA*)

Track: 31mm. Three slim toes, less obviously tapering and spear-shaped than the other large Plover species (see below). No Hallux. Tracks are asymmetrical with toes all slightly different lengths and Toe 4 angled closer to the central toe than is Toe 2. The Metatarsal area registers weakly, if at all, except in softer substrates when the partial webbing between Toes 3 and 4 can also show.

Similar Species: Very difficult to distinguish from the similar-sized Lapwing tracks, which, however, show a Hallux in good substrates. Grey Plover tracks are larger, more robust and with tapering toes.

Notes: Golden Plover and Lapwing often occur together, and on poor substrates their tracks may be inseparable.

Golden Plover tracks, and the impression of a foot in clay.

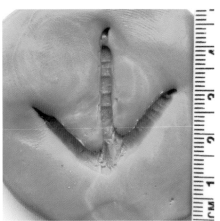

LAPWING (*VANELLUS VANELLUS*)

Track: 30mm. Three slim, spear-shaped toes. The Hallux is present but small and set above the level of the Metatarsal pad. It therefore registers (as just a dot, or a line angled towards the centre of the trail) only in softer substrates. Tracks are asymmetrical with toes all slightly different lengths and Toe 4 angled slightly closer to the central toe than is Toe 2. The Metatarsal area registers weakly, if at all, except in softer substrates when the partial webbing between Toes 3 and 4 can also show. In harder substrates the nails register as separate from the toes.

Similar Species: Very difficult to distinguish from the similar-sized Golden Plover tracks, which, however, never show a Hallux. Grey Plover tracks are larger, more robust and with tapering toes. Compare also with Redshank.

Notes: Lapwing and Golden Plover often occur together, and on poor substrates their tracks may be inseparable.

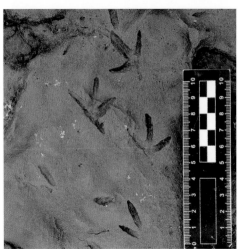

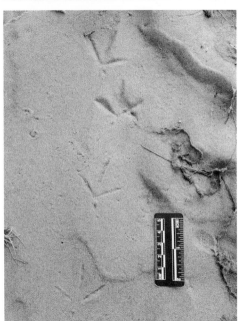

Lapwing tracks and trails showing the large negative space. Also, look carefully for the Hallux 'dot'.

REDSHANK *(TRINGA TETANUS)*

Track: 33mm. Three slim, spear-shaped toes. The Hallux is present but doesn't always show in the track. The Metatarsal area registers weakly, if at all, except in softer substrates when the partial webbing between Toes 3 and 4 can also show.

Similar Species: Very difficult to distinguish from Lapwing tracks, which, however, tend to average smaller and with a relatively shorter Toe 2. Golden Plover and Grey Plover tracks are similar in size but never show a Hallux.

Trails of Redshank (below) and Oystercatcher (above).

Care needs to be taken to identify
Redshank tracks.

GREEN SANDPIPER *(TRINGA OCHROPUS)*

Track: 31mm. Three relatively long, slim but spear-shaped toes. Toe 3 appears to be proportionately longer than in other similar species (see below). The Hallux registers often, set quite far behind the Metatarsal area (which, however, registers weakly if at all). There is partial webbing between Toes 3 and 4, which shows in softer substrates. The angles between the toes seem to vary significantly within any individual trail.

Similar species: Probably inseparable from Wood Sandpiper tracks. The Lapwing has similar-sized tracks but with a shorter Hallux. Golden Plover tracks have no Hallux, and Redshank are on average larger and more robust, but with a short Hallux and proportionately shorter Toe 3.

Notes: Green Sandpiper is a passage and winter visitor in the British Isles (and much of Western Europe), showing a preference for freshwater ditches, pond and river edges, and lakesides where the range of Waders with similar tracks is limited.

Green Sandpiper track drawings showing the variation in toe angles within one trail.

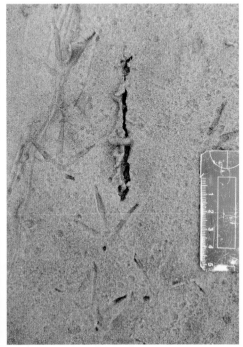

Note the change in toe angles
on these Green Sandpiper tracks.

TURNSTONE (*ARENARIA INTERPRES*)

Track: 28mm. Three relatively long, slim but spear-shaped toes. The Hallux registers often, significantly behind the Metatarsal pad that shows reliably in softer substrates. The tracks are slightly asymmetric. No partial webbing. On harder substrates the Hallux sometimes shows as a dot even when the Metatarsal pad is not showing.
Similar Species: Dunlin have smaller tracks with slimmer toes.

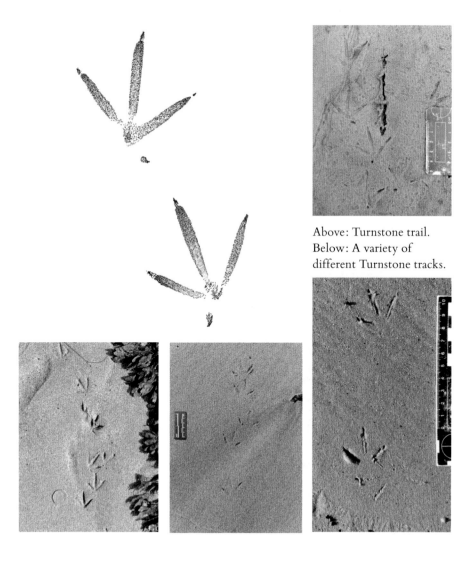

Above: Turnstone trail.
Below: A variety of different Turnstone tracks.

COMMON SANDPIPER (*ACTITIS HYPOLEUCOS*)

Track: 25mm. Very small, with three slim but tapering toes. The tracks are slightly asymmetric, with partial webbing between Toes 3 and 4. The Hallux shows but not reliably, even in soft substrates when the partial webbing shows. The Metatarsal area of the track does not always register.
Similar species: The Little Ringed Plover is smaller, has no Hallux (see Notes) and is more obviously asymmetric.
Notes: Follow a trail of tracks to confirm the presence of the Hallux as an aid to identification. A common track along river banks in breeding areas (which it often shares with Little Ringed Plovers), but also found in tidal creeks on migration.

Common Sandpiper tracks.

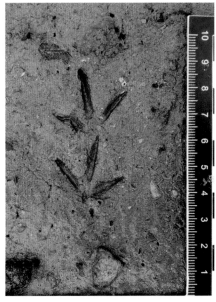

DUNLIN *(CALIDRIS ALPINA)*

Track: 23mm. Very small, with three slender toes. The Hallux shows quite reliably as a small dot. No partial webbing. The tracks appear relatively symmetrical (Toe 4 is slightly closer to the central Toe 3 than Toe 2). The tips of the toes register strongly, and the Metatarsal area weakly, although the Metatarsal pad itself shows often (except when the bird has been running).
Similar Species: Sanderling tracks are even smaller but the toes are broader and spear-shaped. Turnstone tracks are longer and the toes broader.

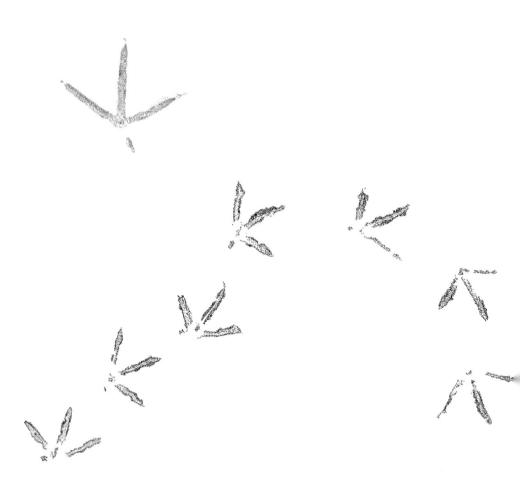

Tracks and trails of Dunlin. Note the trail of the larger Redshank tracks on the second photo.

RINGED PLOVER *(CHARADRIUS HIATICULA)*

Track: 27mm. A small Wader track with three spear-shaped toes. No Hallux. Toes 2 and 4 are held at significantly different angles (*c.*20° difference) from the central Toe 3 making the track obviously asymmetrical. Toe 2 sticks out more to the side whereas Toe 4 hugs closer to the centre. The tips of the toes register strongly (or more deeply) and the Metatarsal area registers lightly, if at all, except in soft substrates when the partial webbing between Toes 3 and 4 may be seen. Ringed Plovers tend to be 'pigeon-toed' with the tracks turning inwards towards the centre of the trail.

Similar Species: Sanderling tracks are similar, but are noticeably smaller and more symmetrical. Specifically, it seems that in Sanderling, Toe 3 is proportionately shorter than the Ringed Plover's, resulting in the toes being more similar in length. Sanderling and Ringed Plovers regularly occur together on beaches.

Notes: Ringed Plovers run regularly, and when they do, Toes 2 and 4 angle closer to the central Toe 3 and the track becomes more symmetrical, and therefore more like Sanderling tracks.

Ringed Plover tracks, obviously asymmetrical.

LITTLE RINGED PLOVER (*CHARADRIUS DUBIUS*)

Track: 19mm. Very small wader track with three spear-shaped toes. No Hallux. As with the larger Ringed Plover, Toes 2 and 4 are held at significantly different angles from the central Toe 3, making the track obviously asymmetrical. Toe 2 sticks out more to the side, whereas Toe 4 hugs closer to the centre. The tips of the toes register strongly (or more deeply) and the Metatarsal area registers lightly, if at all, except in soft substrates when the partial webbing between Toes 3 and 4 may be seen. Little Ringed Plovers tend to be 'pigeon-toed', with the tracks turning inwards towards the centre of the trail.

Similar Species: Very similar to Ringed Plover tracks, but significantly smaller (see Notes). See also Common Sandpiper, which often occurs in similar habitats.

Notes: Little Ringed Plovers are summer visitors and tend to occur at inland wetlands and along slow-flowing sandy or gravelly rivers, which means they rarely occur alongside other species with similar tracks.

Above: A mass of Little Ringed Plover tracks. (MS)

Left: Little Ringed Plover in estuary mud.

SANDERLING (*CALIDRIS ALBA*)

Track: 21mm. Very small with three quite broad spear-shaped toes. No Hallux, and no partial webbing. The tracks appear relatively symmetrical, although Toe 4 hugs slightly closer (*c.*7° closer) to the central Toe 3 than does Toe 2. The tips of the toes register strongly (or more deeply) and the Metatarsal area registers just weakly, if at all, except in soft substrates. Sanderlings run regularly, so tracks can present as just the tips of the toes.
Similar Species: Ringed Plover tracks are similar, but are noticeably larger and more asymmetric. In Ringed Plovers, Toe 3 is proportionately longer, Toe 2 shorter and angled further back than in Sanderling, and the Ringed Plover's Toe 4 is angled closer to the central Toe 3.
Notes: Sanderling tracks are found commonly on sandy beaches, close to the water's edge which is their preferred foraging niche. They often occur in small flocks, running along at the edge of the waves, so tracks and trails can be numerous.

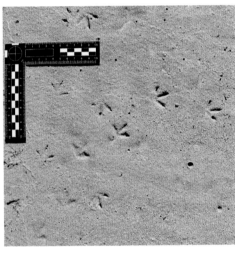

Sanderling tracks and trails.

WOODCOCK (*SCOLOPAX RUSTICOLA*)

Track: 39mm. Three long, slender toes, of which Toe 3 is noticeably the longest and Toe 2 the shortest. The Hallux registers frequently, set quite far behind the Metatarsal area. There is no webbing between the toes. The Metatarsal pad is small but forms a neat dot when it registers in good substrate. The foot is relatively broad across the Metatarsal area.

Similar Species: Difficult to distinguish from Common Snipe tracks, which are structurally very similar although always a little smaller. The Hallux on the Woodcock is longer though, so tends to register further behind the Metatarsal area than in Common Snipe, and the foot is noticeably broader across the Metatarsal than in Snipe. Habitat can be a useful aid in identification.

Notes: A common track in wet woodland, woodland or hedgerow edges, especially in winter (when Woodcock numbers are at their highest).

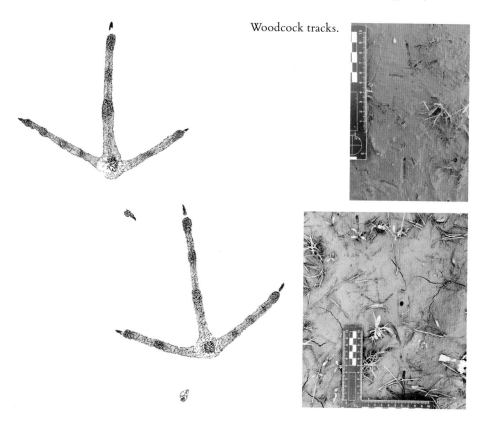

Woodcock tracks.

COMMON SNIPE (*GALLINAGO GALLINAGO*)

Track: 34mm. Three long, slender toes, of which Toe 3 is noticeably the longest, and Toe 2 the shortest. The Hallux registers frequently. There is no webbing between the toes, and a fairly small Metatarsal pad forms a neat dot when it registers in good substrate.

Similar Species: Difficult to distinguish from Woodcock tracks, which have very much the same foot structure although are always a little bigger, and broader across the Metatarsal area. The Hallux is also a bit longer on the Woodcock, so tends to register further behind the Metatarsal area than in Common Snipe. Habitat is a useful aid in identification.

Notes: Common Snipe have a preference for open marshes, bogs, damp meadows and muddy wetlands, and are not normally associated with tree cover (in contrast to Woodcock).

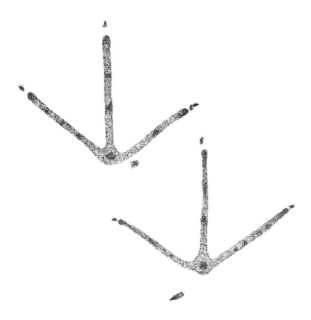

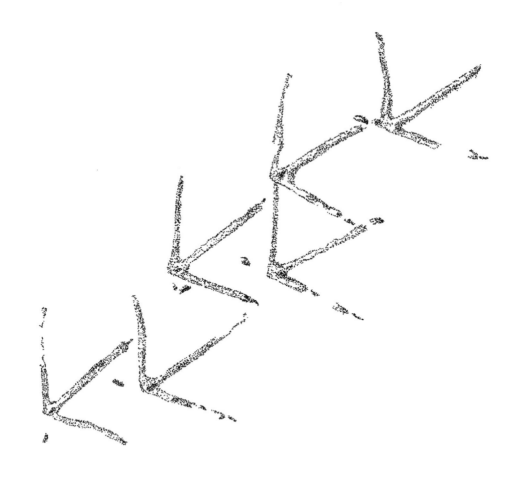

Snipe tracks are very narrow across the Metatarsal area.

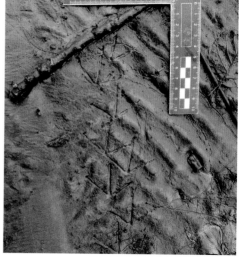

JACK SNIPE (*LYMNOCRYPTES MINIMUS*)

Track: 28mm. We have not found tracks of Jack Snipe, but a freshly dead individual showed it to have an identical foot structure to Common Snipe, only smaller. This track drawing is based on the actual foot for toe lengths (which are consistent with museum specimens), and on the near-identical Common Snipe tracks for toe angles. The actual track may be subtly different, so this is just to highlight the possibility of finding a small 'snipe-like' track in the field.

Notes: Jack Snipe are a numerous winter visitor, albeit a secretive and cryptic one, often frequenting the same habitats as Common Snipe, where their tracks might be found together.

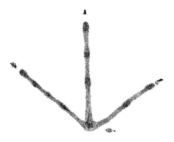

WATER BIRD TRACKS

HERONS AND OTHER LARGE WATER BIRDS

Track type: Classic.
Size: Large to Very Large (96–142mm).
Key features: Long toes, but with variation in Hallux length between species.

SPECIES

White Stork *Ciconia ciconia*
Common Crane *Grus grus*
Great White Egret *Ardea alba*
Grey Heron *Ardea cinerea*
Little Egret *Egretta garzetta*
Cattle Egret *Bubulcus ibis*
Spoonbill *Platalea leucorodia*

LARGE TO VERY LARGE WATER BIRD TRACKS WITH TAPERING TOES AND A REDUCED HALLUX

Both White Stork and Common Crane have a reduced Hallux. In White Stork it is short but registers reliably, whereas with the Common Crane it is even further reduced and doesn't always register in the track. The tapering toes (robust in White Stork and relatively slender in Common Crane) give the look of Wader tracks, and could also be confused with the larger Gamebirds.

LARGE TO VERY LARGE WATER BIRD TRACKS WITH AN OFFSET HALLUX

The Heron family (Herons and Egrets) all have large (or very large) tracks with long, slim toes and a relatively long Hallux that registers reliably. The Hallux has an interesting position in the track, being offset towards the inside. All species have partial webbing between Toes 3 and 4, which is obvious in good substrates.

LARGE WATER BIRD TRACKS WITH SLENDER TOES, A LONG HALLUX AND NOTICEABLE WEBBING

Spoonbills have tracks that are similar to the Herons and Egrets, but their Hallux is in line with Toe 3 (i.e., not offset) and curves slightly towards the centre of the trail. They have a large partial web between Toes 3 and 4, and a smaller one between Toes 2 and 3, which creates a large Metatarsal area. The appearance is more like a small Stork than an Egret.

RAILS

Track type: Classic.
Size: Medium (54–80mm).
Key features: Long slender toes and a short Hallux.

SPECIES

Coot *Fulica atra*
Moorhen *Gallinula chloropus*
Water Rail *Rallus aquaticus*

The Rail family have long slender toes with a Hallux that is significantly shorter than the other toes. The angle that the Hallux presents in tracks seems to be very variable in both Moorhen and Coot. Moorhens have no webbing on the toes, Coots have a fringe of lobate webbing along the edge of all the forward-facing toes. This may show in detail given the right substrate, but often just serves to make the toes look particularly large, fat or ill-defined. Moorhens and Coots are common around inland wetlands and waterways. Water Rail tracks are similar to Moorhen but significantly smaller and with a much-reduced Hallux.

WATER BIRD TRACK DESCRIPTIONS

WHITE STORK *(CICONIA CICONIA)*

Track: 135mm. A very large, classic bird track. Robust, tapering toes, with Toe 2 slightly shorter than Toe 4. Toe 3 is the longest, and the Hallux is relatively short but in line with Toe 3 and registers reliably. There is partial webbing between Toes 3 and 4, which shows in deeper substrates. The Metatarsal pad registers as a circular dot, and does so reliably except in harder substrates.

Similar Species: Common Crane is similar, but smaller with slimmer toes and a much-reduced Hallux.

Notes: White Storks have been the focus of a reintroduction initiative (the White Stork Project), with birds reintroduced in Sussex starting to breed successfully in 2020.

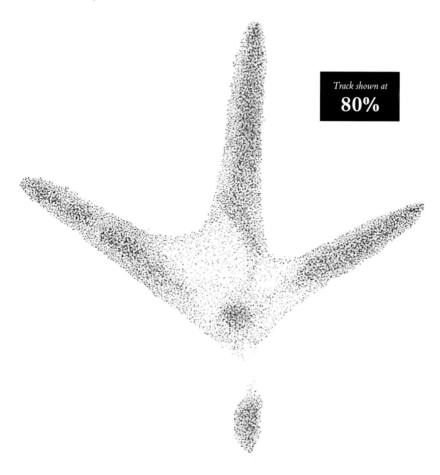

Track shown at
80%

Left: White Stork track. (PN)

Above: Compare the outer toe angle of this White Stork with that of the Common Crane. (AJ)

Right: White Stork trail in loose sand.

COMMON CRANE (*GRUS GRUS*)

Track: 105mm. A large, classic bird track. The Hallux is much reduced and does not always register. The other toes are relatively slim and tapering, with Toes 2 and 4 held out to the sides (more so than in White Stork). There is (a small extent of) partial webbing between Toes 3 and 4. The Metatarsal registers reliably as a circular dot.

Similar Species: Common Crane tracks look like giant Eurasian Curlew tracks. See also White Stork, which is much larger, with more robust toes and a longer Hallux.

Notes: Common Cranes are making a comeback as a breeding species in the British Isles, with over seventy pairs breeding in 2021.

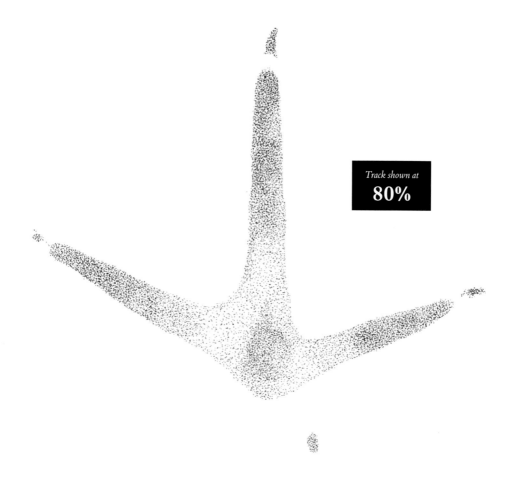

Track shown at
80%

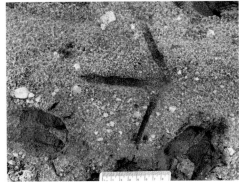

Common Crane tracks.

Common Crane tracks in loose substrate. (MG)

GREAT WHITE EGRET *(ARDEA ALBA)*

Track: 140mm. Large, classic Heron track with long, slim toes that are of an even width along their length. The Hallux (which registers reliably) is offset (to the inside of the track) from the longest toe – Toe 3. The Metatarsal registers weakly (if at all) except in deeper substrates. When it does register, the webbing between Toes 3 and 4 may be seen.

Similar Species: See Grey Heron, which has broader toes and is marginally smaller.

Notes: Track drawn from track photos in Nauta and Pot (2019), and Grolms (2021). We have not seen these tracks in the field. Great White Egrets are increasing in number in Britain and are now a regular breeding species.

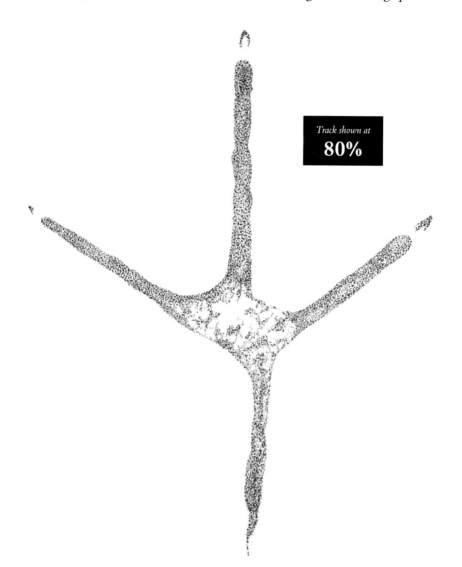

Track shown at
80%

Great White Egret tracks showing the classic offset Hallux that is characteristic of the Heron family. (RN)

GREY HERON (*ARDEA CINEREA*)

Track: 135mm. Large, classic Heron track. Long, relatively slim toes that are of an even width along their length. The Hallux (which registers reliably) is offset (to the inside of the track) from the longest toe – Toe 3. The Metatarsal registers weakly (if at all) except in deeper substrates. When it does register, the webbing between Toes 3 and 4 may be seen.
Similar Species: The Great White Egret has slimmer toes, which may or may not be obvious depending on substrate. The tracks of the other egrets are significantly smaller. Compare with other large species such as White Stork, which has more robust, tapering toes and a shorter Hallux, and White-tailed Eagle, which has robust toes with large bulbous toe pads and long claws.

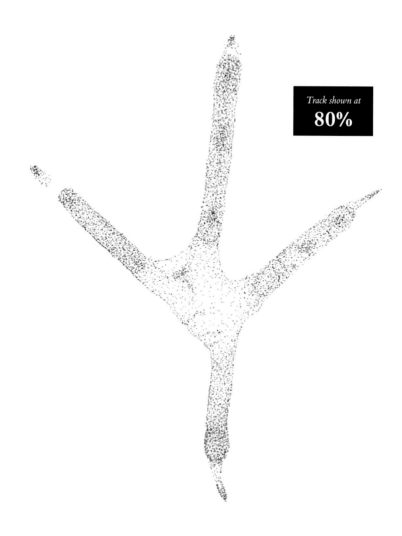

Track shown at
80%

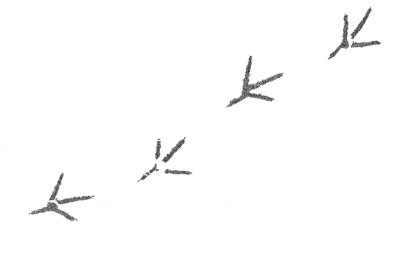

Grey Heron track in soft mud.

Grey Heron trail in snow.

LITTLE EGRET (*EGRETTA GARZETTA*)

Track: 96mm. Small, classic Heron track with long, slim toes that are of an even width along their length. The Hallux (which registers reliably) is offset (to the inside of the track) from the longest toe – Toe 3. The Metatarsal registers weakly (if at all) except in deeper substrates. When it does register, the webbing between Toes 3 and 4 may be seen.
Similar Species: Grey Heron has broader toes and is larger.
Notes: When walking fast, the tracks of Little Egret can become narrower with Toe 2 moving in closer to Toe 3 – hugging it – making the track look like a huge, slim-toed Crow track.

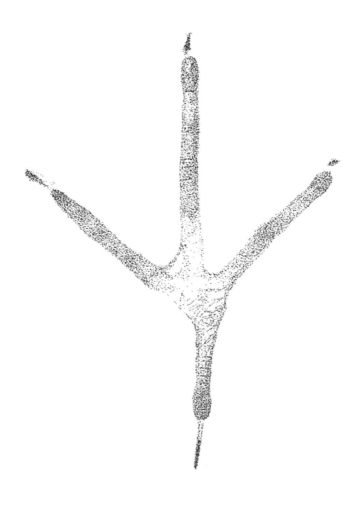

Little Egret track (with a Carrion Crow above).

Little Egret trail in soft mud.

CATTLE EGRET (*BUBULCUS IBIS*)

Track: 100mm. Small, classic Heron track with long, slim toes that are of an even width along their length. The Hallux (which registers reliably) is offset (to the inside of the track) from the longest toe – Toe 3. The Metatarsal registers weakly (if at all) except in deeper substrates. When it does register, the webbing between Toes 3 and 4 may be seen.

Similar Species: Compared with the Little Egret, the toes of the Cattle Egret appear slightly more robust, the Hallux proportionately longer, and Toe 2 proportionately shorter, making the track look long and narrow.

Notes: Track drawn from track photos in Abenza García (2018), and Nauta and Pot (2019). Cattle Egrets are increasing in number in Britain and are now starting to breed regularly.

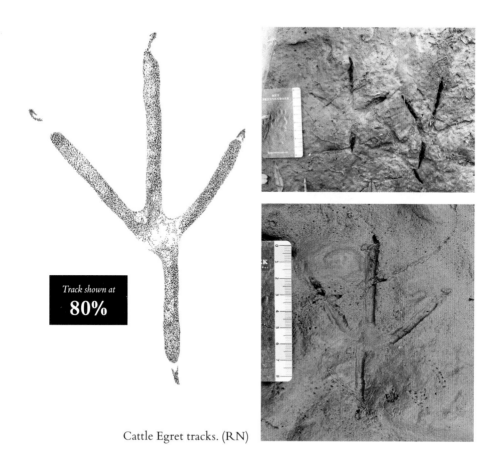

Track shown at **80%**

Cattle Egret tracks. (RN)

SPOONBILL (*PLATALEA LEUCORODIA*)

Track: 120mm. Heron-like, and with slim toes but the Hallux is in line with Toe 3, and there is a large partial web between Toes 3 and 4 and a smaller (but noticeable) web between Toes 2 and 3. The Metatarsal area tends not to register, or at least does not register as deeply as the toes. The webbing does show in the tracks.
Similar Species: Compare with the smaller egrets.
Notes: Track drawn from track photos in Abenza García (2018), Nauta and Pot (2019), and Grolms (2021). Spoonbills are increasing in number in southern England and are now a regular breeding species.

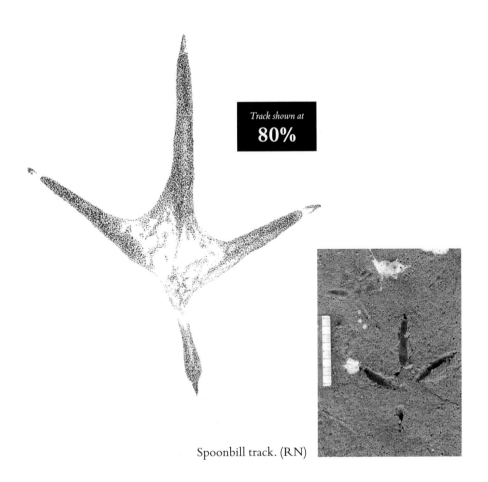

Spoonbill track. (RN)

EURASIAN COOT (*FULICA ATRA*)

Track: 80mm. Long, relatively slender toes. Toe 3 tends to bend towards the centre of the trail. The toes are fringed with lobate webbing that can show in the right substrate but often just makes the toes look indistinct or poorly defined. The angle at which the Hallux registers is variable.
Similar Species: Common Moorhen tracks have straight toes and no hint of webbing.

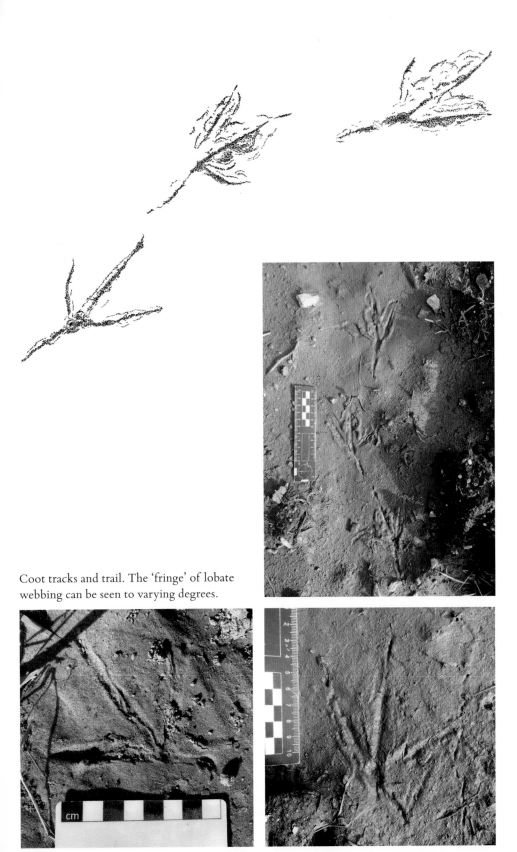

Coot tracks and trail. The 'fringe' of lobate webbing can be seen to varying degrees.

COMMON MOORHEN (*GALLINULA CHLOROPUS*)

Track: 74mm. Long, straight toes that tend to register more deeply than the Metatarsal, although the whole foot registers reliably, as does the long Hallux. The toes can sometimes appear spear-shaped depending on substrate. Track size ranges from 70 to 80mm (due to sexual dimorphism). The position of the Hallux in the track is highly variable (from almost in line with Toe 3 to being at right angles with Toe 3).

Similar Species: The Eurasian Coot has very similar toes that don't always show the lobed webbing in the tracks. The toes are, however, often not as straight as those of the Moorhen.

Notes: A common track beside any body of water (lakes, ponds, rivers, marshes).

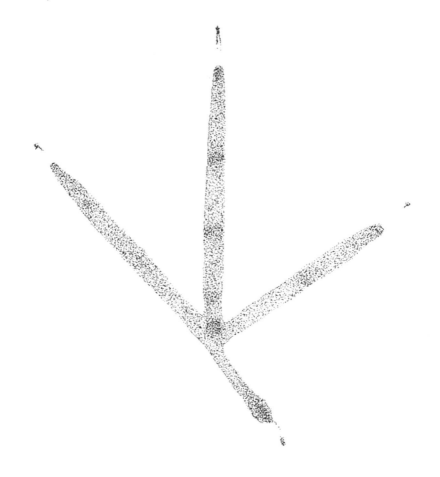

Moorhen tracks and trails.

WATER RAIL (*RALLUS AQUATICUS*)

Track: 54mm. Typical Rail track with long, slender toes, but with a short Hallux (*c.*10mm long).

Similar Species: Smaller tracks than the similar Common Moorhen. Compare also with Woodcock.

Notes: Track drawn from the foot impression in Bergmann and Klaus (2016), a foot photo in Nauta and Pot (2019), with toe angles informed by those of Moorhen and the closely related Virginia Rail (*Rallus limicola*) from Elbroch and Marks (2001). Track size is approximate.

WEB-FOOTED
BIRD TRACKS

Web-footed birds have an Anisodactyl foot structure, very similar to Gamebirds and Waders, with three toes pointing forwards and a much-reduced Hallux pointing backwards. All of the Web-footed bird groups are 'palmate' – they have full webbing between Toes 2 and 3, and between Toes 3 and 4. A small number of bird species have full-length webbing between all four toes and are termed Totipalmate. The webbing extends, more or less, to the ends of the toes and the shape of the leading edge of this webbing (either concave or straight) can help in narrowing down your track to a particular group of birds. With all the Web-footed bird groups it often happens that the webbing will not show in the track – the level of detail found being totally dependent on the substrate. Without the webbing showing it is easy to confuse these species with Gamebirds and Waders.

SWANS, GEESE AND DUCKS

The Swans, Geese and Ducks all have full webbing between their forward-facing toes. Look closely at Toes 2 and 4, which are almost always curved in these groups, straighter in Gulls and Terns and totally straight in Gamebirds and Waders. It might be useful to imagine the web like a piece of latex pulling these toes in towards the central Toe 3. Depending on the group, Toe 2 is shorter than the others, which impacts the symmetry although these groups tend to look more symmetrical than the Gulls and Terns. When the webbing is present in the track look closely at the distal edge, which may be more or less either straight or slightly concave depending on the group. It is possible in some cases to recognise the usually shorter inner Toe 2 from the webbing angle. In some species (some Ducks and Geese) there is an extra flange of webbing on the outer edge of Toe 2. This extra webbing varies in width depending on species but has the effect of making this toe look extra fat or wide in the track, and often poorly defined. Where present, this is a good feature for separating tracks from those of the Gulls. Another key feature to look for in the Swans, Geese and Ducks is the Metatarsal pad, which registers reliably as a circle (of varying size). The Hallux in these birds is much reduced but may register strongly and regularly, only occasionally or not at all depending on species.

Due to the variation in track sizes between the sexes and across the age range of these species, and the inconsistent presentation of webbed feet in different substrates, we currently believe that it is not possible to separate similar-sized Geese and Duck species reliably by their tracks alone. The same is true of similar-sized Swan species.

The young of these webbed birds leave the nest soon after hatching and are therefore abroad on the landscape long before their feet are fully grown. For example, we have found tiny Duck tracks around a woodland pond in the late spring – the tracks were the size of Eurasian Teal but belonged to 'still growing' Mallard. So, keep in mind that Cygnets, Goslings and Ducklings will have significantly smaller feet than the adults and will all be confusable with the adult feet of other Web-footed species.

SWANS

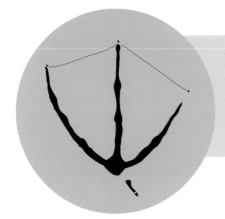

Track type: Fully webbed.
Size: Large to Very Large (132–160mm).
Key features: Long, slender toes.
Small Metatarsal area. Straight edge
to the webbing.

SPECIES

Mute Swan *Cygnus olor*
Whooper Swan *Cygnus cygnus*
Black Swan *Cygnus atratus*

There are four species of Swan that may be encountered in the British Isles. The Mute Swan is our largest species, is resident year-round and will be the most likely Swan tracks you'll encounter. Whooper and Bewick's Swans migrate each winter to our shores from the high Arctic. Bewick's Swan is the smallest Swan. The fourth species – the Black Swan – is originally from Australia and was introduced here as an ornamental species. They are increasingly found in the wild in the southern half of Britain.

Compared with other Web-footed birds, Swan tracks are enormous, especially the Mute Swan, which generally precludes them from being confused with even the largest Geese. However, there may well be a size crossover between the largest Geese and the Bewick's Swan. It's also worth keeping in mind that recently hatched Cygnets will leave significantly smaller tracks than their parents.

Considering the size of the tracks, Swan toes are relatively slender and delicate in appearance. Toe 2 is the smallest, resulting in a fairly steep angle of the webbing from the end of Toe 3. Toe 4 is almost as long as the central Toe 3 and the distal edge of the webbing is generally straight with little concavity on both sides of the track. Nails show reliably in the tracks. It's worth noting that the extra flange of webbing present on Toe 2 on some species of Geese and Duck tracks is not present in the Swans.

Swans have a relatively small Metatarsal area considering the overall size of the track, but it can register strongly as a circular dot. The Hallux is much reduced and will register only in the softest of substrates. It may not be able to separate Swans to species level with complete confidence!

GEESE

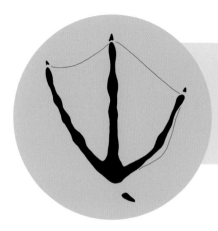

Track type: Fully webbed.
Size: Large (63–105mm).
Key features: Long, robust toes. Toe 2 with flange of webbing in some species. Straight edge to the webbing.

SPECIES

White-fronted Goose *Anser albifrons*
Greylag Goose *Anser anser*
Barnacle Goose *Branta leucopsis*

Pink-footed Goose *Anser brachyrhynchus*
Canada Goose *Branta canadensis*
Brent Goose *Branta bernicla*

The Geese mark a crossover between the larger Ducks and smaller Swans, especially in terms of the size of their tracks, but also with many features common to both groups. However, and with exception of the Bewick's Swan, Geese are significantly smaller than swans. The toes in Geese tracks are, in most cases, robust and the nails show reliably. Like the Swans, Toe 4 is almost as long as the leading central Toe 3. Toe 2 is the shortest, causing a steep angle at the distal edge of the webbing connected to Toe 3. Between the leading toe and Toe 4 this webbing angle is flatter.

The webbing is relatively straight-edged (slightly concave in some species). In some species of Geese, the inner Toe 2 can appear broader due to an additional flange of webbing along the edge of the toe that forms a narrow flap. This is variable in width depending on species and is also present (to varying extents) and more commonly in the Ducks, but not in Swans. The Metatarsal area registers reliably as a dot in all but the hardest substrates, and the Hallux also shows well, substrate permitting.

DUCKS

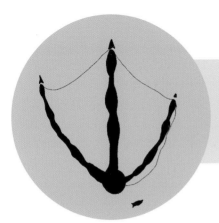

Track type: Fully webbed.
Size: Medium to Large (42–79mm).
Key features: Long outer toes. Straight edge to the webbing.

SPECIES

Shelduck *Tadorna tadorna*

Eider *Somateria mollissima*

Pintail *Anas acuta*

Shoveler *Spatula clypeata*

Pochard *Aythya ferina*

Smew *Mergellus albellus*

Egyptian Goose *Alopochen aegyptiaca*

Mallard *Anas platyrhynchos*

Eurasian Teal *Anas crecca*

Wigeon *Mareca penelope*

Red-breasted Merganser *Mergus serrator*

Mandarin Duck *Aix galericula*

In the Ducks, Toes 2 and 4 are closer in length when compared to the small Geese. The central Toe 3 is still the longest, and Toe 4 next, but Toe 2 is closer to it in length. This alters the general appearance of the track, making it look more symmetrical. This symmetry is transferred to the angle of the distal end of the webbing, making it more even on both sides of the leading Toe 3. The Metatarsal area registers well, as does the Hallux in good substrate (although this varies between species). The toes are relatively robust, especially so at the joints. Nails often register reliably in the tracks, although their significance is variable. In most cases Duck tracks are broad in relation to their length and can be as wide as they are long.

Ducks can be split into two groups: the Dabbling Ducks, such as Mallard, that feed on the surface or from the surface, and Diving Ducks that dive to seek their food under water (such as Pochard and Red-breasted Merganser). The Diving Ducks follow the basic Dabbling Duck features outlined above but they seem to have an even longer Toe 4, and the tracks can appear narrower in relation to their length (such as in Pochard), although this doesn't appear to be consistent across Diving Duck species. For example, the Red-breasted Merganser we have found were in fact quite wide (contrary to e.g., Brown et al., 2013). Egyptian Goose and Shelduck are included here as they are most closely related to the Ducks rather than Geese.

SWANS, GEESE AND DUCKS TRACK DESCRIPTIONS

MUTE SWAN (*CYGNUS OLOR*)

Track: 160mm. Huge, webbed track. Toes are long and slender with broader areas at the toe joints. Toes 2 and 4 curve in slightly. Nails are short but often register. The track is slightly asymmetrical, with Toe 2 marginally shorter than Toe 4. The Metatarsal pad registers strongly, and the Hallux is long and slender, but is not always obvious in the tracks.
Similar Species: Probably indistinguishable from the similar-sized Whooper Swan. The other Swans are smaller, with all the Geese species smaller still.

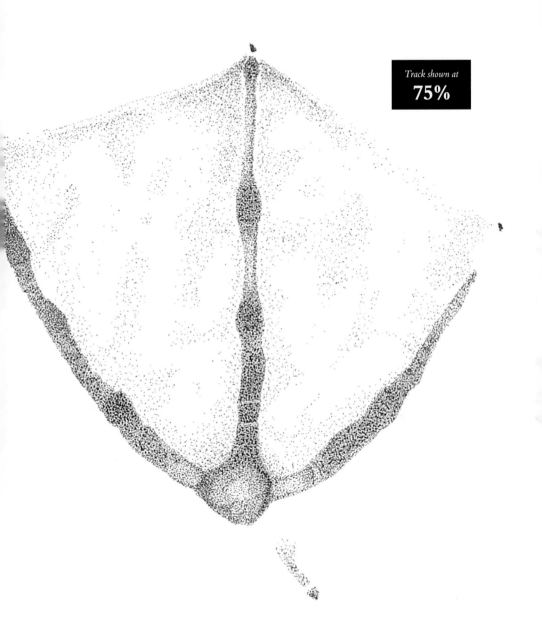

Track shown at
75%

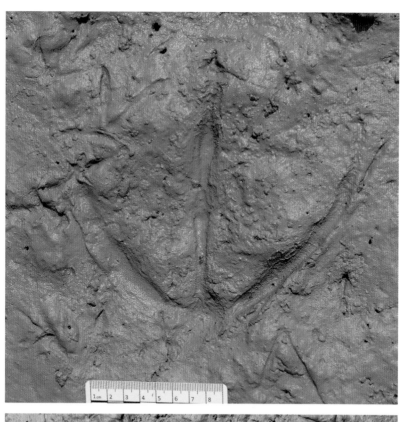

Mute Swan tracks.

WHOOPER SWAN (*CYGNUS CYGNUS*)

Track: 158mm. Huge, webbed track with all the same features as Mute Swan. The Hallux registers only occasionally.
Similar Species: Probably indistinguishable from Mute Swan. The other Swans are smaller, with all the Geese species smaller still.

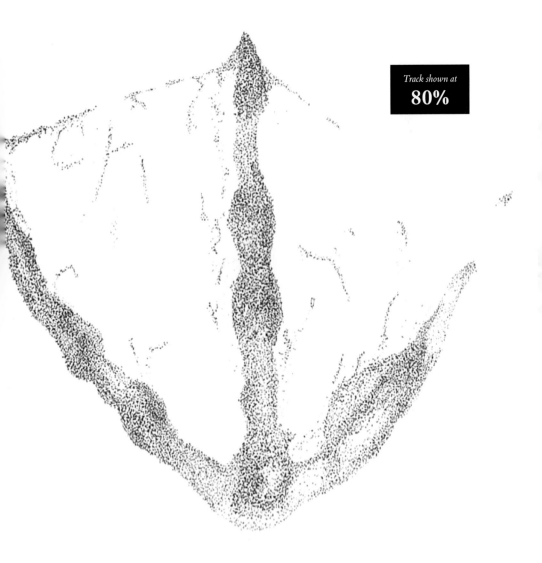

Track shown at
80%

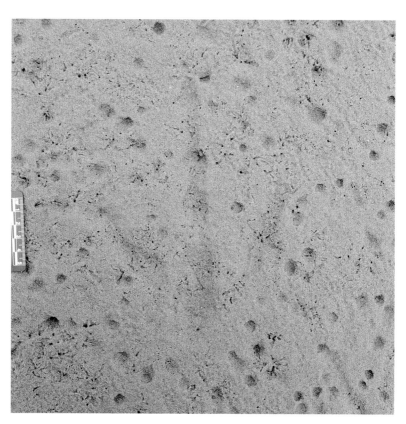

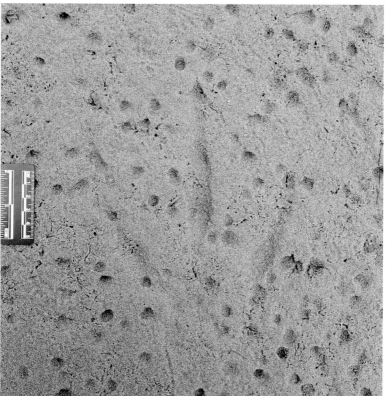

Whooper Swan tracks.

BLACK SWAN *(CYGNUS ATRATUS)*

Track: 132mm. Huge, webbed track with all the same features as Mute Swan. The Hallux registers only occasionally.

Similar Species: Mute Swan and Whooper Swan tracks are larger. Probably indistinguishable from similar-sized Bewick's Swan, although we have not seen their tracks. Tracks of the Geese species are all smaller.

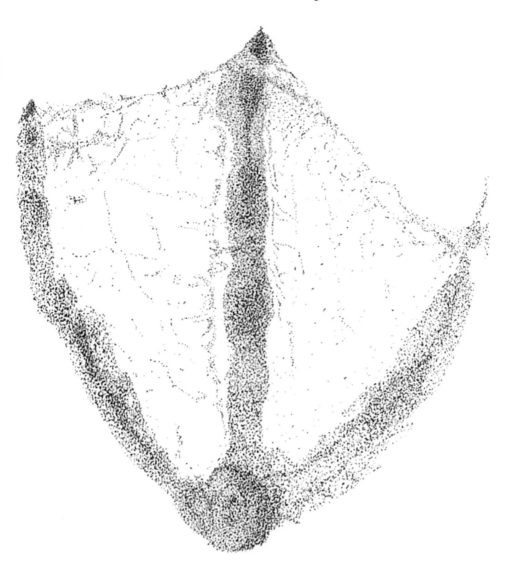

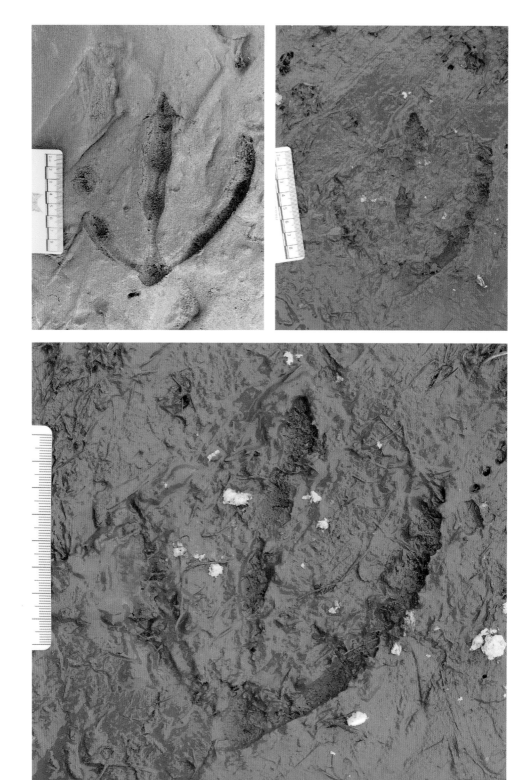

Black Swan tracks in different quality substrates.

CANADA GOOSE (*BRANTA CANADENSIS*)

Track: 105mm. Large track made by our largest goose. The toes appear to be more slender than in the other large Geese, but are robust at the toe joints. Toes 2 and 4 curve inwards slightly. Toe 2 has a wide (*c*.5mm) flap of webbing on its outside edge, which can make Toe 2 look robust. The Metatarsal pad registers clearly, and the Hallux is long and slender, but only occasionally registers.

Similar Species: Greylag Goose is very similar, but smaller (although there could be overlap when considering sexual dimorphism). Compare also with the larger tracks of Swans.

Notes: Along with Greylag Goose, the tracks of the Canada Goose are the most commonly encountered large, webbed track.

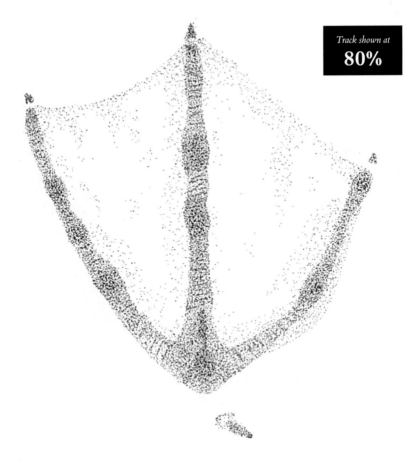

Track shown at
80%

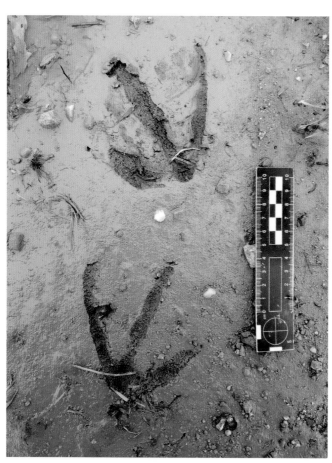

Canada Goose tracks.

GREYLAG GOOSE (*ANSER ANSER*)

Track: 91mm. Large, robust Goose track. Toes 4 appears to be relatively straight. Toe 2 has a wide flap of webbing on its outside edge which makes Toe 2 look especially broad. The Metatarsal pad registers strongly, and the Hallux is long and slender, but does not reliably register.

Similar Species: Canada Goose tracks are very similar, and although they average 10 per cent larger, there could be overlap when considering sexual dimorphism. Compare with the medium-sized Geese species.

Notes: Along with Canada Goose, the tracks of Greylag are the most commonly encountered large, webbed track.

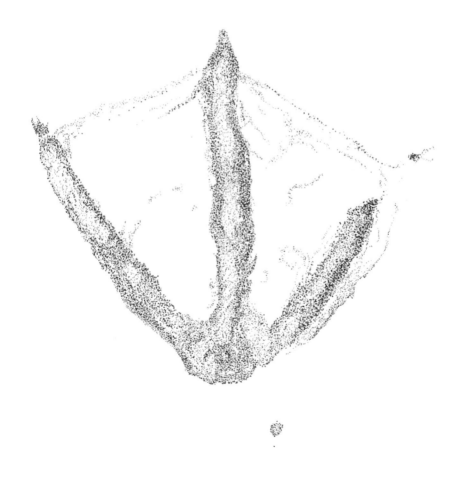

 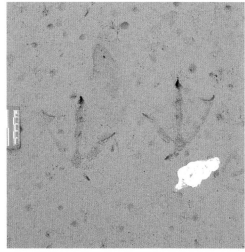

Greylag Goose with barely any
evidence of webbing.

Greylag Goose track with the webbing
clearly visible.

WHITE-FRONTED GOOSE *(ANSER ALBIFRONS)*

Track: 82mm. Medium-sized Goose track. The toes are relatively robust, especially so at the toe joints. Nails register in good substrate. The track is slightly asymmetrical with Toe 2 shorter than Toe 4. Toe 2 has a flap of webbing on its outside edge (*c.*5mm wide), which makes Toe 2 look especially broad. The Metatarsal pad registers strongly, and the Hallux is long and slender, but does not always register.

Similar Species: Probably indistinguishable from the Pink-footed Goose. Compare with the larger Greylag Goose.

Notes: White-fronted Geese are winter visitors to the British Isles and tend to occur in large, single-species flocks.

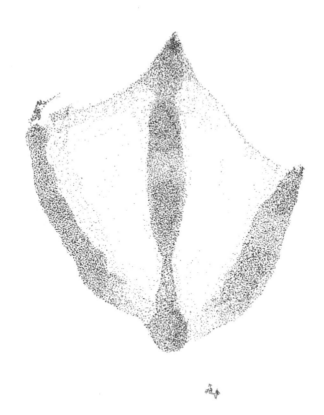

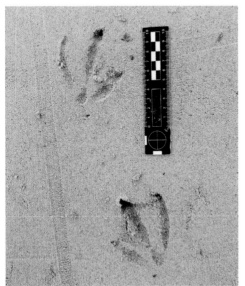

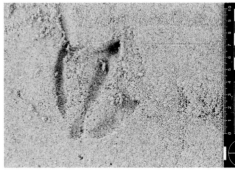

Note the 'pigeon-toed' aspect of these White-fronted Goose tracks.

PINK-FOOTED GOOSE (*ANSER BRACHYRHYNCHUS*)

Track: 80mm. Medium-sized Goose track that is essentially identical to that of the White-fronted Goose. Toe 2 has just a narrow flap of webbing on its outside edge (*c.*2mm wide). The Hallux is long and slender, but only occasionally registers.

Similar Species: Probably indistinguishable from the White-fronted Goose. Compare with the larger Greylag Goose.

Notes: Pink-footed Geese are winter visitors to the British Isles and tend to occur in large, single-species flocks.

Pink-footed Goose tracks. (DP)

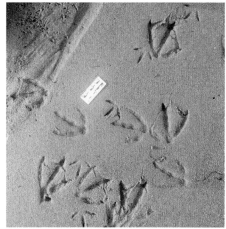

EGYPTIAN GOOSE (*ALOPOCHEN AEGYPTIACA*)

Track: 79mm. Medium-sized Goose track. Robust toes (especially so at the toe joints). Nails are long and noticeable. The track is asymmetrical, with Toe 2 shorter than Toe 4. These toes are relatively straight (just a gentle curve inwards) and can be held quite wide. Toe 2 has a wide flap of webbing on its outside edge which makes the toe look especially broad. The Metatarsal pad is large and registers strongly. The Hallux is robust for a goose and tends to register reliably.

Similar Species: The other medium-sized Geese have slightly less robust toes, less obvious nails, smaller Metatarsal pads and register a smaller Hallux (if it registers at all).

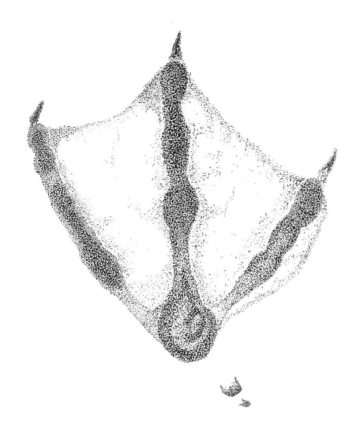

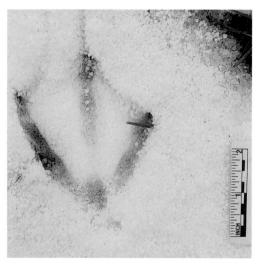

Egyptian Goose tracks in snow.

Egyptian Goose tracks in soft mud.

BARNACLE GOOSE (*BRANTA LEUCOPSIS*)

Track: 68mm. Small Goose track with especially robust toes. Nails register in good substrate. The track is slightly asymmetrical, with Toe 2 shorter than Toe 4. Toe 2 has just a narrow flap of webbing on its outside edge. The Metatarsal pad is large and registers as a big circle. The Hallux only registers occasionally.
Similar Species: More robust and with a larger Metatarsal pad than the Brent Goose. Compare also with the large Duck species.
Notes: A winter visitor, forming large flocks in coastal areas, primarily in the north although there are some feral breeding flocks across England.

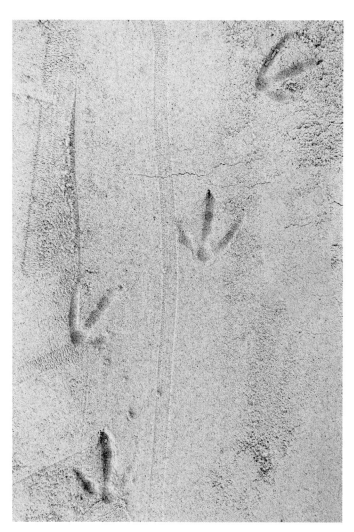

Barnacle Goose tracks in soft sand.

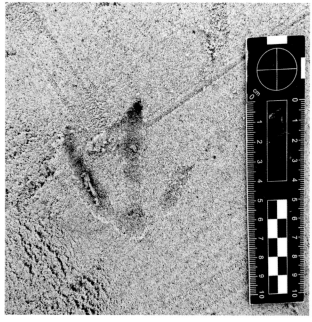

BRENT GOOSE (*BRANTA BERNICLA*)

Track: 63mm. Small, but noticeably wide Goose track. Nails register in good substrate. The track is slightly asymmetrical with Toe 2 shorter than Toe 4. Toe 2 has just a narrow flap of webbing on its outside edge. The Metatarsal pad registers clearly. The Hallux registers unpredictably.

Similar Species: Less robust and with a smaller Metatarsal pad than the Barnacle Goose. Proportionately wider tracks than the large Duck species.

Notes: A Goose of coastal salt marsh, grazing marsh, tidal estuaries and adjacent beaches. Consider habitat and location when identifying a track.

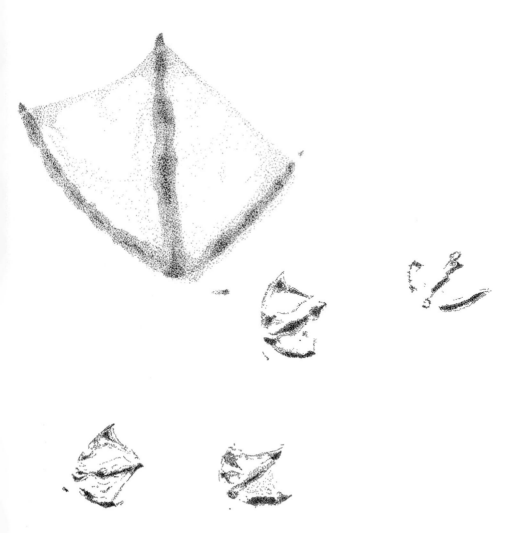

Brent Goose tracks in estuary mud.

Brent Goose tracks in sand.

EIDER (*SOMATERIA MOLLISSIMA*)

Track: 83mm. Our largest Duck, leaving huge (Goose-sized) tracks. Toe 4 is proportionately longer than in other ducks, and almost equal in length to Toe 3, which gives the tracks a unique symmetry. The front edge of the webbing is straight or just slightly concave. The Metatarsal pad is relatively small and registers often (but not always). The Hallux is long, vertically flattened (like a rudder) and registers some of the time. When it does, it leaves a line close to the base of Toe 2. Toe 2 has a wide (8–10mm) flap of webbing on its outside edge, which can make the toe look especially broad.

Similar Species: Compare with the similar-sized Geese (noting relative toe lengths and symmetry).

Notes: Eiders regularly loaf on beaches and leave long trails as they move in and out of the sea. Like all Ducks, Eiders are sexually dimorphic, with females noticeably smaller than males. In the case of Eiders, females leave tracks averaging 79mm, and males 86mm.

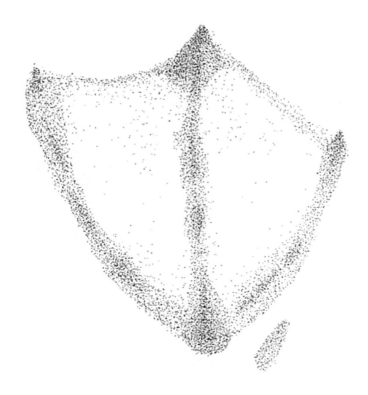

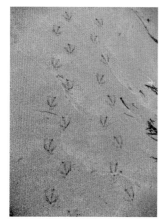
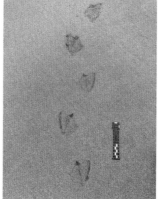

Parallel trails of Eider.   Eider tracks made by ducks and drakes.

RED-BREASTED MERGANSER (*MERGUS SERRATOR*)

Track: 73mm. A very large Duck track. The toes appear to be held quite wide while walking, and the front edge of the webbing is straight or just slightly concave. The Metatarsal pad is small and registers some of the time. The Hallux also registers some of the time. Toe 2 has a wide flap of webbing on the outside edge, which can make the toe look particularly broad.

Similar Species: There are very few similar-sized Ducks, but compare with Eider, the smaller Geese and the larger Gulls.

Notes: Red-breasted Mergansers often loaf on beaches and can leave long trails as they move in and out of the sea.

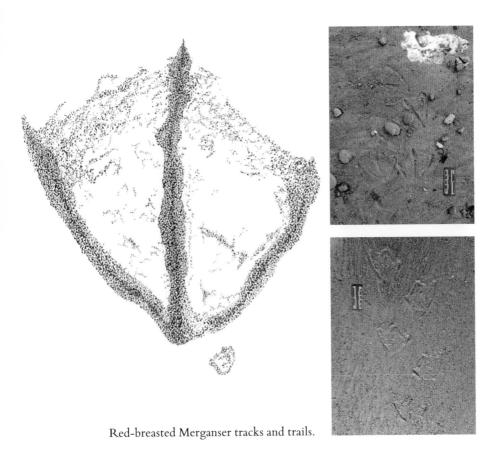

Red-breasted Merganser tracks and trails.

SHELDUCK (*TADORNA TADORNA*)

Track: 68mm. Large Duck track with robust toes. Asymmetrical with Toe 2 shorter than Toe 4, but with both of these toes curving inwards along their length. Toe 2 has a flap of webbing on its outside edge, making Toe 2 look particularly broad. The Metatarsal pad registers clearly, and the Hallux registers reliably.

Similar Species: Compare with the slightly smaller Mallard and the small Geese. Tracks of the large gulls are webbed and of a similar size but don't show the Hallux.

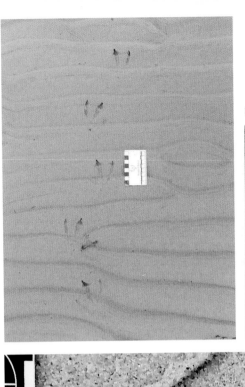

Shelduck tracks and trails in various substrates.

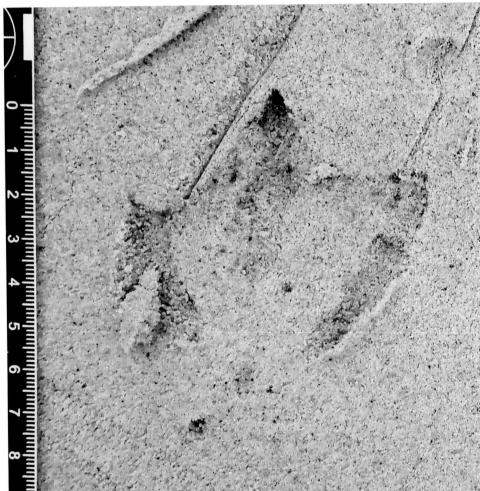

MALLARD (*ANAS PLATYRHYNCHOS*)

Track: 63mm. A large and typical Duck track. Slightly asymmetrical (with Toe 2 the shortest, and Toe 3 the longest). The toes are enlarged (or 'lobed') at the joints (especially Toe 3). As with most ducks, the Hallux and Metatarsal pad register reliably, as do the nails. Toe 2 has a wide flap of webbing on its outside edge, which makes the toe look especially broad.
Similar Species: Other similar-sized Ducks leave very similar (possibly inseparable) tracks. Gull tracks tend not to show the Hallux.
Notes: The most commonly encountered Duck track.

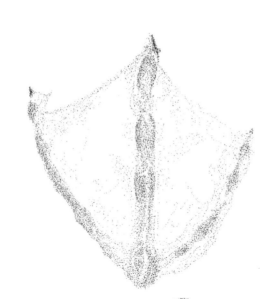

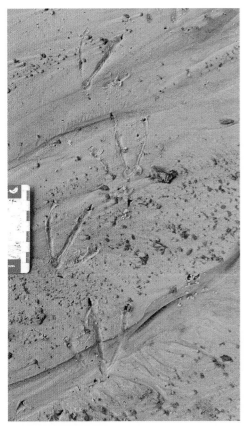

Mallard tracks.

PINTAIL (*ANAS ACUTA*)

Track: 59mm. Typical Duck track with the Hallux, Metatarsal pad and nails registering relatively reliably. The flap of webbing on the outside edge of Toe 2 is narrower than in Mallard but is still present and does make the toe look broad.

Similar Species: Other similar-sized Ducks leave very similar (possibly inseparable) tracks. Gull tracks tend not to show the Hallux.

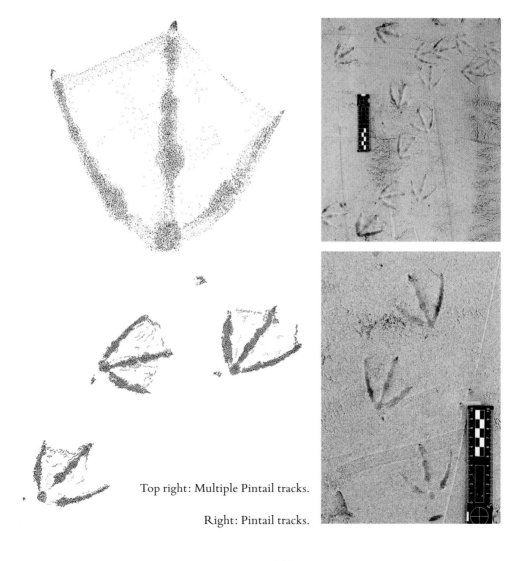

Top right: Multiple Pintail tracks.

Right: Pintail tracks.

WIGEON (*MARECA PENELOPE*)

Track: 56mm. Typical Duck track with the Hallux, Metatarsal pad and nails registering relatively reliably. The Hallux is proportionately shorter than in other similar-sized Ducks. The flap of webbing on the outside edge of Toe 2 is narrow but is still present and can make the toe look broad. There seems to be a tendency for Wigeon tracks to have noticeably curved Toes 2 and 4.

Similar Species: Other similar-sized ducks leave very similar (possibly inseparable) tracks, although notice the overall track shape and length of Hallux as these may represent identifiers. Gull tracks tend not to show the Hallux.

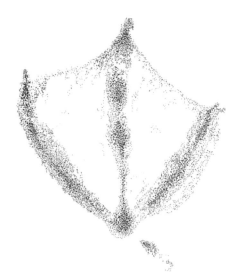
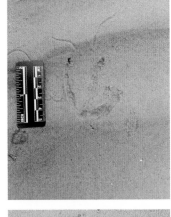

Wigeon tracks in mud and sand.

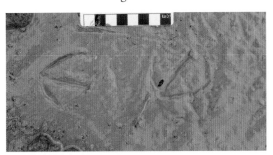
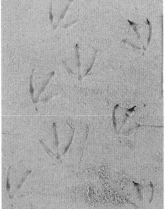

SHOVELER (*SPATULA CLYPEATA*)

Track: 54mm. Typical Duck track with the Hallux, Metatarsal pad and nails registering relatively reliably. The Hallux is proportionately longer than other similar-sized Ducks. The flap of webbing on the outside edge of Toe 2 is narrower than in the Mallard but is still present and can make the toe look broad. The overall impression is of a relatively straight-sided (Toes 2 and 4) track.

Similar Species: Other similar-sized Ducks leave very similar (possibly inseparable) tracks. Gull tracks tend not to show the Hallux.

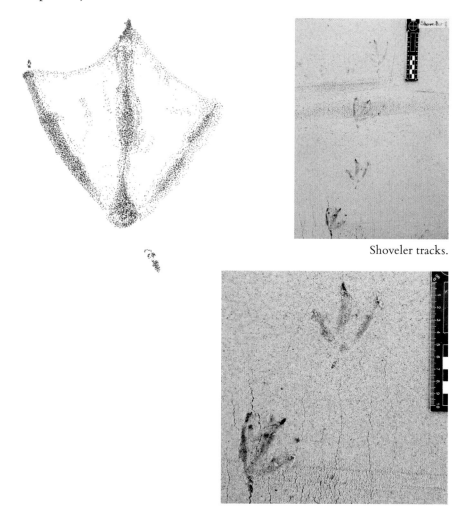

Shoveler tracks.

POCHARD *(AYTHYA FARINA)*

Track: 55mm. A typical Duck track, although the overall appearance is of a more slender track due to Toe 4 being held a little closer to Toe 3 than in other Ducks. The flap of webbing on the outside edge of Toe 2 is narrow.
Similar Species: The smaller Tufted Duck has the same Toe 2 webbing flap and a similar-length Hallux (determined from museum specimens) and probably leaves similar tracks, although we have not found these.
Notes: Drawing and description based on just one track.

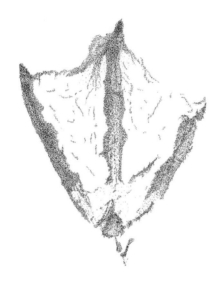

MANDARIN DUCK (*AIX GALERICULATA*)

Track: 54mm. Typical Duck track with the Hallux and Metatarsal pad registering reliably. Toe 2 has a wide flap of webbing on the outside edge that can make the toe look particularly broad.

Similar Species: Probably inseparable from other similar-sized Ducks, but the nails are possibly more prominent and the toes more robust than in other Ducks.

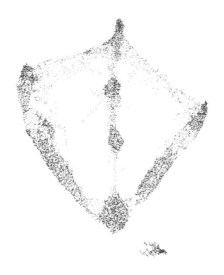

Mandarin Duck tracks.

SMEW (*MERGELLUS ALBELLUS*)

Track: 53mm. Typical Duck track. The Metatarsal pad is relatively small but registers reliably. The Hallux is long but doesn't show in all tracks. Smew have no flap of webbing on Toe 2.

Similar Species: Other similar-sized Ducks are possibly inseparable. Compare with Gull tracks.

Notes: A scarce winter visitor to the British Isles, and the tracks of these wintering birds are unlikely to be found. The species is, however, kept in waterfowl collections.

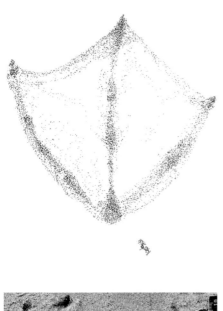

Smew tracks in sand.

EURASIAN TEAL (*ANAS CRECCA*)

Track: 42mm. Our smallest Duck, leaving the smallest Duck tracks. The Metatarsal pad does not always show in the track. In the trails we have found, the Hallux registers about 50 per cent of the time. Nails register. There is just a narrow flap of webbing on the outside of Toe 2.
Similar Species: Other duck species are larger. Compare with the similar-sized Black-headed Gull and Common Gull. Keep in mind the possibility (during the breeding season) of tracks made by ducklings of larger species.

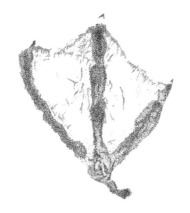

Eurasian Teal tracks and trail.

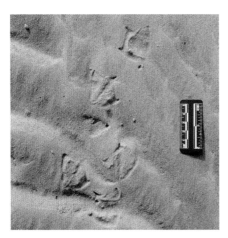

GULLS AND TERNS

All the Gulls, Terns and Skuas tend to walk 'pigeon-toed' – with their feet turned in towards the centre of the trail, although not in such an extreme manner as the Ducks (with which these species could be confused). None of the Gulls or Terns have the extra flap of skin on Toe 2 that makes this toe look so fat in some Duck and Geese species. This same toe is also proportionately shorter in the Gulls and Terns (causing greater asymmetry) than in the Ducks. More specific details and differences are described below.

GULLS

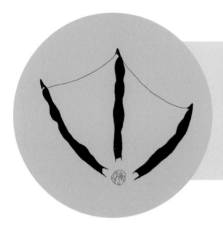

Track type: Fully webbed.
Size: Medium to Large (39–75mm).
Key features: Metatarsal pad shows some of the time. Hallux greatly reduced and rarely shows. Concave edge to the webbing.

SPECIES

Arctic Skua *Stercorarius parasiticus*
Great Black-backed Gull *Larus marinus*
Lesser Black-backed Gull *Larus fuscus*
Herring Gull *Larus argentatus*
Common Gull *Larus canus*
Black-headed Gull *Chroicocephalus ridibundus*
Kittiwake *Rissa tridactyla*

Gull tracks are asymmetrical, with central Toe 3 the longest, the outer Toe 4 almost as long but the inner Toe 2 quite obviously the shortest (and proportionately shorter than with most Duck species). The toes tend to be straighter than with the Ducks, and the edge of the webbing more concave. The Metatarsal pad registers some of the time (in about 50 per cent of tracks for the medium-sized Gulls according to Elbroch and Marks, 2001). The Hallux in Gulls is set quite high up on the 'ankle' and therefore only registers in deeper substrates. Track size varies considerably from the largest Great Black-backed Gull to the small Common and Black-headed Gulls. The tracks of Arctic Skua, by comparison, are more symmetrical with Toes 2 and 4 very similar in length, and they are more likely to register the Metatarsal pad and the Hallux than the Gulls.

TERNS

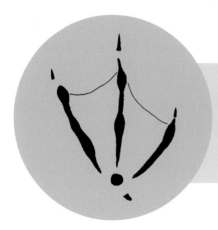

Track type: Fully webbed.
Size: Small (19–28mm).
Key features: Long Toe 3 (with a long nail). Nails and Hallux show. Concave edge to the webbing.

SPECIES

Sandwich Tern *Thalasseus sandvicensis*
Common Tern *Sterna hirundo*
Arctic Tern *Sterna paradisaea*
Little Tern *Sternula albifrons*

Tern tracks are in many ways structurally similar to the smaller Gulls, but the central Toe 3 is noticeably longer than the others, the impression of which is accentuated by an especially long nail that registers in the track. Toe 3 is prominent beyond the webbing, which is deeply concave along the distal edge. The Metatarsal area shows more reliably than in most Gull tracks, as does the Hallux. All the nails register well.

GULLS AND TERNS TRACK DESCRIPTIONS

ARCTIC SKUA *(STERCORARIUS PARASITICUS)*

Track: 44mm. A unique track among the Gulls and Terns. Almost symmetrical with Toes 2 and 4 relatively long, similar in length, and only just a little shorter than Toe 3. The Metatarsal pad registers (even if just slightly), as does the Hallux.
Similar Species: Similar in size to the Common Gull, which has more robust toes, lacks the symmetry and does not show a Hallux. The Black-headed Gull is smaller, asymmetrical and lacks the Hallux.
Notes: Most likely to be found on beaches close to the northern isles breeding grounds.

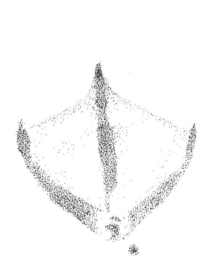

Arctic Skua tracks in sand.

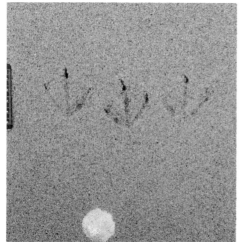

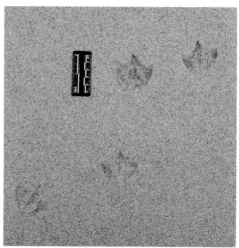

GREAT BLACK-BACKED GULL (*LARUS MARINUS*)

Track: 75mm. A typical, webbed, large Gull track with Toe 3 obviously longer than the toes either side, and Toe 4 noticeably longer than Toe 2. Nails on each toe often register, and do so ahead of the webbing (if this is visible). The Hallux is greatly reduced, sitting behind the Metatarsal and up the 'ankle', so only shows in deeper substrates. The Metatarsal pad appears to register – albeit lightly.

Similar Species: Averages larger than the Herring Gull and Lesser Black-backed Gull, but otherwise identical and considering size variation it may not be possible to distinguish between these big Gulls. Compare with the smaller Geese and larger Ducks.

Notes: Track length is based on one individual.

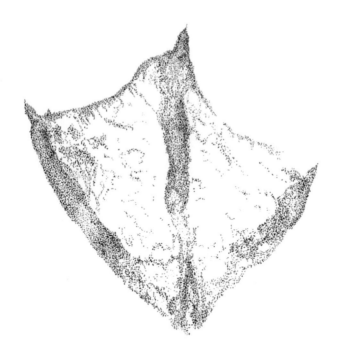

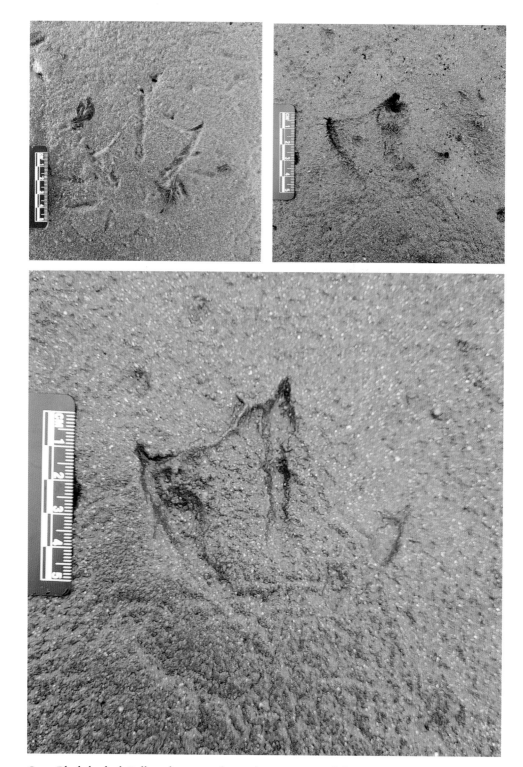

Great Black-backed Gull tracks – note the weak registration of the Metatarsal area. The Metatarsal pad registers in about 50 per cent of tracks of these large Gulls.

LESSER BLACK-BACKED GULL (*LARUS FUSCUS*)

Track: 60mm. A typical, webbed, large Gull track. Toes 2 and 4 appear to be relatively straight, and the webbing (if visible) only slightly concave. Nails on each toe often register. The Hallux is greatly reduced, so only shows in deeper substrates. The Metatarsal pad, which is relatively small, appears to register – albeit lightly.

Similar Species: Averages larger than the Herring Gull and smaller than the Great Black-backed Gull, but otherwise identical, and considering size variation it may not be possible to distinguish between these big Gulls. Compare with the smaller Geese and larger Ducks.

Notes: Track length is based on tracks from one individual.

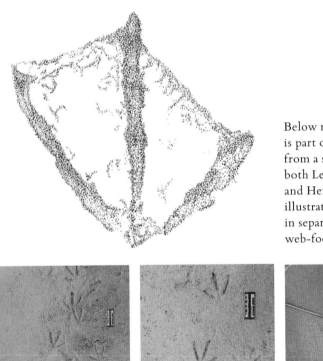

Below right: This trail is part of a set of tracks from a small flock of both Lesser Black-backed and Herring Gulls, and illustrates the difficulty in separating similar-sized web-footed birds.

  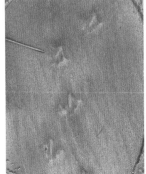

Left and middle: Lesser Black-backed Gull tracks.

HERRING GULL (*LARUS ARGENTATUS*)

Track: 64mm. A typical, webbed, large Gull track, with Toe 3 obviously longer than the toes either side, and Toe 4 noticeably longer than Toe 2. Nails on each toe often register, and do so ahead of the webbing (if this is visible). The Hallux is greatly reduced, sitting behind the Metatarsal and up the 'ankle', so only shows in deeper substrates. The Metatarsal pad appears to register (at least lightly) in most tracks.

Similar Species: Averages smaller than the Black-backed Gull, but considering size variation it may not be possible to distinguish between the tracks of these big Gulls. Compare with the smaller Geese and larger Ducks.

Herring Gull foot.

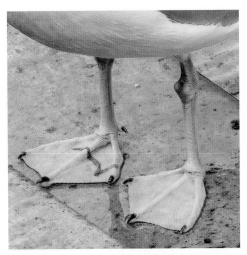

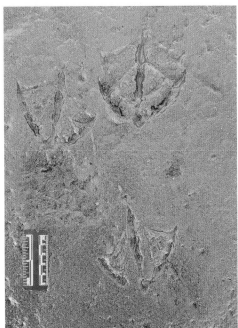

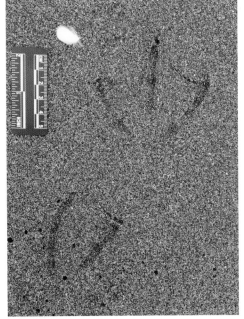

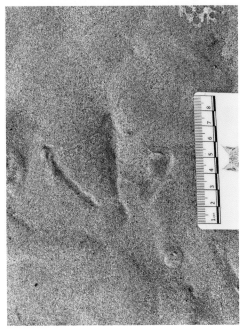

Herring Gull feet, and tracks in various substrates.

COMMON GULL (*LARUS CANUS*)

Track: 45mm. A typical, webbed, medium-sized Gull track, with Toe 3 obviously longer than the toes either side, and Toe 4 noticeably longer than Toe 2. Nails sometimes register (ahead of the webbing). The Hallux is greatly reduced, sitting behind the Metatarsal and up the 'ankle', so only shows in deeper substrates. The Metatarsal pad appears to register some of the time (see Notes).

Similar Species: Noticeably smaller than the large Gulls. The Black-headed Gull is smaller. Compare with the small Ducks.

Notes: Elbroch and Marks (2001) found that about half of the medium-sized Gull tracks they analysed showed the Metatarsal pad.

Common Gull tracks.

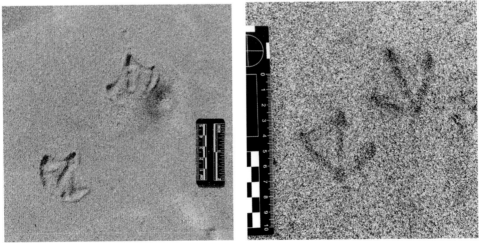

KITTIWAKE (*RISSA TRIDACTYLA*)

Track: 50mm. A very delicate but medium-sized Gull track with slender toes. The nails seem to register beyond the ends of the toes. The Hallux is greatly reduced and unlikely to register. The Metatarsal pad appears to register as a circular spot.

Similar Species: Larger but more delicate than the Black-headed Gull. Compare with the small Ducks.

Notes: Primarily a pelagic species, so the tracks are only likely to be found around breeding colonies. Information based on a small number of tracks.

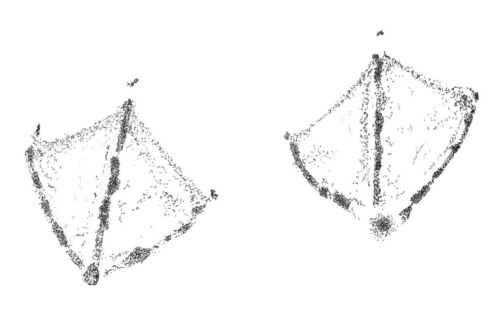

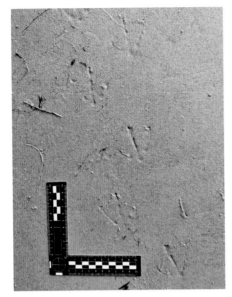
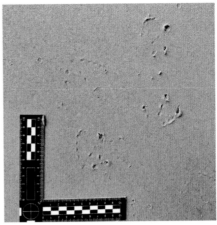

Kittiwake tracks showing contrasting levels of detail.

BLACK-HEADED GULL
(*CHROICOCEPHALUS RIDIBUNDUS*)

Track: 39mm. The smallest Gull track likely to be found, and typical of the group, albeit with slender toes and the Metatarsal pad registering lightly (if at all).

Similar Species: Closest to the Common Gull, but smaller and more delicate. Compare with the smallest Duck species.

Notes: Elbroch and Marks (2001) found that about half of the medium-sized Gull tracks they analysed showed the Metatarsal pad, and this seems to hold true for the Black-headed Gull.

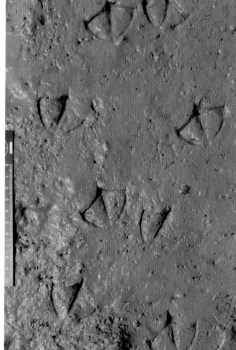

Black-headed Gull trails and tracks.

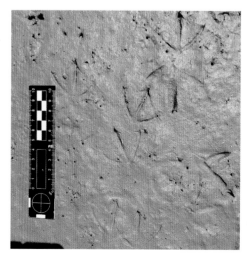

SANDWICH TERN (*STERNA SANDVICENSIS*)

Track: Approx. 28mm. The largest Tern track. Toe 3 is noticeably longer than the other toes, with the toe pad extending beyond the webbing. A long nail (about 6mm) on Toe 3 further accentuates its length. The Hallux and Metatarsal pad show reliably in the tracks.

Similar Species: The other Terns are just a few millimetres smaller and may not be separated reliably in the field. Compare also with Gull tracks, which are much larger and don't show the Hallux and Metatarsal as reliably.

Notes: Drawn from a track photo in Nauta and Pot (2019), and checked against specimens in the British Museum of Natural History. The photo this was drawn from had no scale, so the track size is approximate but informed by measurements from museum skins.

Sandwich Tern tracks. (GK)

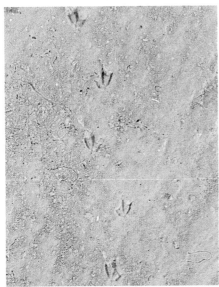

COMMON TERN *(STERNA HIRUNDO)*

Track: 25mm. As with all the Terns, Toe 3 is noticeably longer than the other toes, with the toe pad extending beyond the webbing. A long nail on Toe 3 further accentuates its length. The Hallux and Metatarsal pad show reliably in the tracks.

Similar Species: The tracks are, on average, just 2mm longer than those of Arctic Tern and therefore probably not separable in the field. Where Common and Arctic Terns have been resting on the beach together, it has not been possible to distinguish between their tracks. The Little Tern is smaller. Compare also with the much larger Gull tracks.

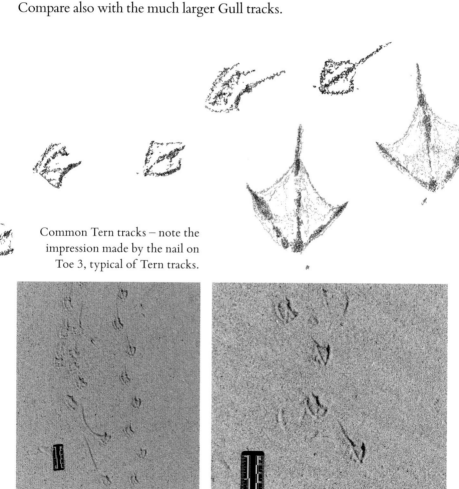

Common Tern tracks – note the impression made by the nail on Toe 3, typical of Tern tracks.

ARCTIC TERN (*STERNA PARADISAEA*)

Track: 23mm. Arctic Tern tracks are essentially identical to those of the Common Tern, for a description of which see above. Averaging just 2mm shorter, these two species are probably inseparable in the field.

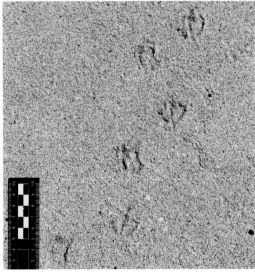

Arctic Tern tracks on a challenging tracking substrate.

LITTLE TERN (*STERNULA ALBIFRONS*)

Track: 19mm. Tiny. The smallest Tern tracks. Toe 3 is noticeably longer than the other toes, with the toe pad extending beyond the webbing. A long nail (4–5mm) on Toe 3 further accentuates its length. The Hallux and Metatarsal pad show reliably in the tracks.

Similar Species: The other Tern species are much larger.

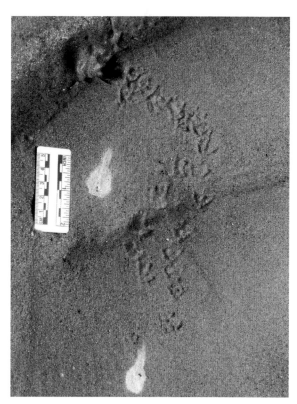

Little Tern trail as it walked away from a resting spot.

TOTIPALMATE

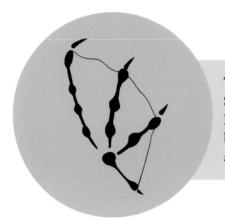

Track type: Totipalmate.
Size: Very large (131–135mm).
Key features: Webbing present between the Hallux, Toe 2, Toe 3 and Toe 4.

SPECIES

Great Cormorant *Phalacrocorax carbo*
Northern Gannet *Morus bassanus*

Part of the Web-footed birds group, the Totipalmate species have a long and reliably registering Hallux. They are also webbed not only between the three forward-facing toes but also between the Hallux and Toe 2. In the British Isles this Totipalmate arrangement is found only on Cormorants, Shags and Gannets.

TOTIPALMATE TRACK DESCRIPTIONS

GREAT CORMORANT *(PHALACROCORAX CARBO)*

Track: 131mm. These Totipalmate tracks are unique in terms of symmetry. Toe 4 is longest and forms a long sweeping curve with the Hallux, which shows reliably (even if just the nail). The Metatarsal pad shows reliably. The toes are robust and the toe joints register, even on hard substrates. While there is webbing between each of the toes, this often does not show in the tracks, especially the web between the Hallux and Toe 2. Cormorants walk but will increase speed to take flight and move to a hopping gait, registering just Toes 2, 3 and 4, and eventually just the nails of these toes before they are airborne.

Similar Species: The closely related European Shag is smaller and will therefore have near-identical but smaller tracks. However, the Shag is a bird of rocky coasts, so rarely stands on substrates where tracks will be left. See Northern Gannet, and compare with geese and swan tracks.

Notes: Cormorants rest regularly on sandy beaches, muddy banks or lake sides (often drying their wings after fishing), so their tracks (and obvious whitewash scat) can be found regularly in these places.

Great Cormorant trail.

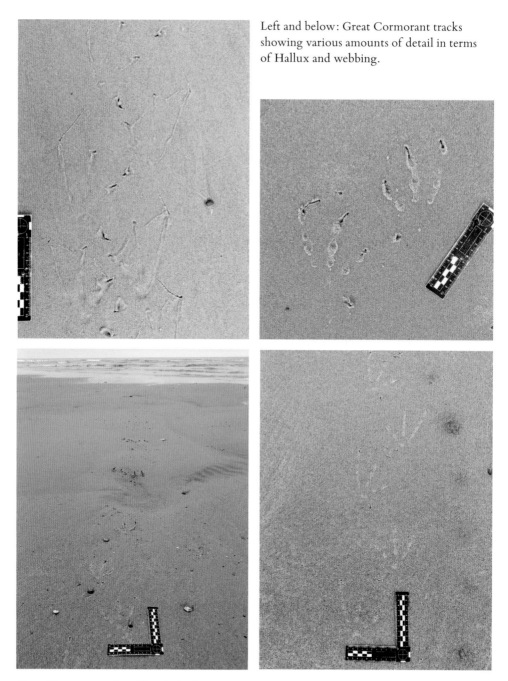

Left and below: Great Cormorant tracks showing various amounts of detail in terms of Hallux and webbing.

Great Cormorant take-off trail. As they gather speed, Cormorants make big hops – feet together and three toes (or rather nails) registering.

NORTHERN GANNET (*MORUS BASSANUS*)

Track: 135mm. Totipalmate, with Toe 4 the longest (marginally longer than Toe 3) and forming a long sweeping curve with the Hallux, which shows reliably, as does the Metatarsal pad. While there is webbing between each of the toes, this is not clear in the tracks, especially the web between the Hallux and Toe 2.

Similar Species: Great Cormorant tracks are marginally smaller, the toes more robust and by far the more likely to be found.

Notes: This track was drawn from a trail of one moribund individual walking on a Shetland beach in 2022. It was infected with the Avian Influenza (Bird Flu) virus that was decimating the Gannet population there at the time. Gannets rarely walk unless grounded by extreme strong winds or through injury and sickness, so their tracks will be a rare occurrence and most often the bird that left them will be present.

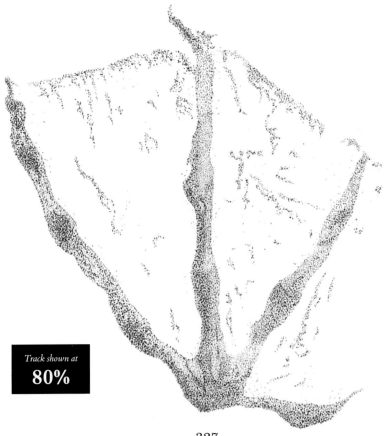

Track shown at
80%

327

Northern Gannet tracks. Gannets don't spend much time on the ground, so their tracks are a rare find.

REFERENCES AND RESOURCES

Abenza García, L. (2018), *Aves que dejan huella*. Madrid: MADbird Nature Watching Fair.

Baker, N. (2013), *The RSPB Nature Tracker's Handbook*. London: Bloomsbury.

Bergmann, H-H. and Klaus, S. (2016), *Spuren und Zeichen de Vögel Mitteleuropas*. Wiebelsheim, Germany: AULA-Verlag.

Brown, R., Ferguson, J., Lawrence, M. and Lees, D. (2013), *Tracks and Signs of the Birds of Britain and Europe*. Second Edition. London: Christopher Helm.

Burton, N.H.K. and Armitage, M.J.S. (2005), 'Differences in the diurnal and nocturnal use of intertidal feeding grounds by Redshank *Tringa totanus*', *Bird Study* 52: 120–128.

Van Diepenbeek, A. (2019), *Veldgids: Diersporen Europa*. Zeist, Netherlands: KNNV Uitgeverij.

Elbroch, M. and Marks, E. (2001), *Bird Tracks and Sign: a guide to North American species*. Pennsylvania, USA: Stackpole Books.

Grolms, J. (2021), *Tier Spuren Europas: Spuren und Zeichen bestimmen und interpretieren*. Stuttgart, Germany: Eugen Ulmer KG.

Nauta, R. and Pot, A. (2019), *Het Prentenboek*. Vledder, Netherlands: EXTRA Uitgeverij.

Olsen, L-H. (2013), *Tracks and signs of the animals and birds of Britain and Europe*. Princeton, USA: Princeton University Press.

Parkin, D.T., Collinson, M., Helbig, A.J., Knox, A.G. and Sangster, G. (2003), 'The taxonomic status of Carrion and Hooded Crows', *British Birds* 96(6): 274–290.

Puplett, D. (2019), *Guide to British Bird Tracks and Signs*. Telford, UK: Field Studies Council.

Rhyder, J. (2021), *Track and Sign: a guide to the field signs of mammals and birds of the UK*. Cheltenham, UK: The History Press.

Snow, D.W. and Perrins, C.M. (eds) (1998), *The Birds of the Western Palearctic* (Concise Edition). Oxford, UK: Oxford University Press.

Svensson, L., Mullarney, K. and Zetterström, D. (2009), *Collins Bird Guide*. Second Edition. London: HarperCollins.

INDEX

Species illustrated and described in this book have a dedicated section in **bold**.